Hávamál
(The Sayings of the High One)

Original Text, Translations, and Word Lists

Translated by
Matthew Leigh Embleton

Copyright ©2025 Matthew Leigh Embleton. All rights reserved.

Hávamál (The Sayings of the High One)

Hávamál (The Sayings of the High One)..4
Word List *(Old Norse to English)*..49
Word List *(English to Old Norse)* 73

Cover: Old Norse text over an outline of Odin and Sleipnir. Author's design.

The original Old Norse text is in the public domain.
This translation ©2021 Matthew Leigh Embleton
©2025 Matthew Leigh Embleton (This Edition)

Acknowledgments

I have long been fascinated by languages and history, and I am very grateful to the special people in my life who have supported and encouraged me in my work. Thank you for believing in me. You know who you are.

Introduction

The Hávamál ('The Sayings of the High One' i.e. 'Odin') is a collection of poetry from the Viking age. It can be described as 'gnomic poetry' in that it contains a series of insightful verses which offer advice in the form of maxims and aphorisms (short statements, observations, and opinions) about how to live one's life, how to conduct oneself in a proper manner, and how to gain and use wisdom in order to survive and prosper in a dangerous world.

Old Norse is a North Germanic language spoken by inhabitants of Scandinavia from about the 7th to the 15th centuries.

The text is presented in its original Old Norse, with a literal word-for-word line-by-line translation, and a Modern English translation, all side-by-side. In this way, it is possible to see and feel how the Old Norse language worked and how it has evolved. Also included is a word list with 1,471 Old Norse words translated in to English, and 1,148 English words translated into Old Norse.

This book is designed to be of use and interest to anyone with a passion for the Old Norse or Old Icelandic language, Old Norse history, or languages and history in general.

Hávamál (The Sayings of the High One)

Hávamál (The Sayings of the High One)

	Old Norse	Literal	English

I.

1

	Gáttir allar,	Gates all,	All gates,
	áðr gangi fram,	before going forward,	Before going forward,
	um skoðask skyli,	about look should,	One should look about,
	um skyggnast skyli,	around peer should,	And one should peer around,
	því at óvíst er at vita,	for that uncertain is to know,	Because it is uncertain to know,
	hvar óvinir	where enemies	Where enemies
	sitja á fleti fyrir.	sit on bench before.	Sit on benches inside.

2

	Gefendr heilir!	Givers hail!	Hail to the givers!
	Gestr er inn kominn,	Guest has in come,	A guest has come in,
	hvar skal sitja sjá?	where shall sit see?	Where shall the stranger sit?
	Mjök er bráðr,	Much is haste,	He is much in haste,
	sá er á bröndum skal	he who to firewood shall	Who to the firewood shall,
	síns of freista frama.	his of try luck.	Try his luck.

3

	Elds er þörf,	Fire is needed,	Fire is needed,
	þeims inn er kominn	he in has come	He has come in,
	ok á kné kalinn;	and about knees frozen;	And about his knees are frozen,
	matar ok váða	food and clothes	Food and clothes,
	er manni þörf,	are man's need,	Are a man's need,
	þeim er hefr um fjall farit.	they who have about mountains fared.	Those who have fared about mountains.

4

	Vatns er þörf,	Water is needed,	Water is needed,
	þeim er til verðar kemr,	they who to meal comes,	For those that come to a meal,
	þerru ok þjóðlaðar,	towel and hospitality,	A towel and hospitality,

Hávamál (The Sayings of the High One)

	Old Norse	Literal	English
	góðs of æðis, ef sér geta mætti, orðs ok endrþögu.	good of mood, if he get may, words and silence.	Good of words, He may get if, He speaks and is silent.
5	Vits er þörf, þeim er víða ratar; dælt er heima hvat; at augabragði verðr, sá er ekki kann ok með snotrum sitr.	Wits are needed, they who widely roam; easy is home what; for eye-mockery becomes, he who nothing knows and with the-wise sits.	Wits are needed, By those whom roam widely; It is easy at home; For mockery comes to, He who knows nothing, And sits among wise men.
6	At hyggjandi sinni skyli-t maðr hræsinn vera, heldr gætinn at geði; þá er horskr ok þögull kemr heimisgarða til, sjaldan verðr víti vörum, því at óbrigðra vin fær maðr aldregi en mannvit mikit.	In thought his shouldn't man boastful be, rather wary in mind; then when wise and silent comes home-yard to, seldom becomes misfortune to-the-wary, for that unfailing friend gets man never than man-sense much.	In his thoughts, A man should not be boastful, But rather wary in mind; And then wise and silent, Who comes to the home yard, Rarely does misfortune come to the wary, For that unfailing friend, A man never gets better than, Wisdom that is true.
7	Inn vari gestr, er til verðar kemr, þunnu hljóði þegir, eyrum hlýðir, en augum skoðar; svá nýsisk fróðra hverr fyrir.	The wary guest, who to meal comes, tuned hearing silent, ears listen, and eyes look; so informed wise-men every for.	The wary guest, Who comes to a meal, Tune his hearing and be silent, Listen with his ears, And look with his eyes, Every informed and wise man does this.

Hávamál (The Sayings of the High One)

	Old Norse	Literal	English
8			
	Hinn er sæll,	One is happy,	One is happy,
	er sér of getr	who himself about gets	Who gets for himself,
	lof ok líknstafi;	praise and regard;	Praise and regard;
	ódælla er við þat,	uneasy is with that,	Uneasy is that,
	er maðr eiga skal	which man owns shall	Which a man owns,
	annars brjóstum í.	another's breast in.	In another's heart.
9			
	Sá er sæll,	One is happy,	One is happy,
	er sjalfr of á	who himself of has	Who has for himself,
	lof ok vit, meðan lifir;	praise and wit, while lives;	Praise and wit, while he lives;
	því at ill ráð	since that ill advice	Since ill advice,
	hefr maðr oft þegit	has man often received	Have men often received,
	annars brjóstum ór.	another's breast from.	From another man's heart.
10			
	Byrði betri	Burden better	A better burden,
	berr-at maðr brautu at	bears-not man his-way on	Can no man bear on his way,
	en sé mannvit mikit;	than so man-sense much;	Than much wisdom;
	auði betra	riches better than	Better than riches,
	þykkir þat í ókunnum stað;	seems that in unknown land;	It seems in an unknown land;
	slíkt er válaðs vera.	such as needy being.	To be such in need.
11			
	Byrði betri	Burden better	A better burden,
	berr-at maðr brautu at	bears-not man his-way on	Can no man bear on his way,
	en sé mannvit mikit;	than so man-sense much;	Than much wisdom;
	vegnest verra	wares worse	And no worse
	vegr-a hann velli at	carry-not he plains on	Can he carry on the plains,
	en sé ofdrykkja öls.	than being over-drinking ale.	Than too big a drink of ale.

Hávamál (The Sayings of the High One)

	Old Norse	Literal	English

12

| | Er-a svá gótt
sem gótt kveða
öl alda sona,
því at færa veit,
er fleira drekkr
síns til geðs gumi. | Not as good
as good quoted
ale of-men's sons,
since that less knows,
who more drinks
his about mind man. | Not as good,
As is well said,
Is ale for men's sons,
Since they know less,
They who drink more,
Of their own mind. |

13

| | Óminnishegri heitir
sá er yfir ölðrum þrumir,

hann stelr geði guma;
þess fugls fjöðrum
ek fjötraðr vark
í garði Gunnlaðar. | Forgetful-heron called
that which over ale-party hovers,

it steals mind man's;
this bird's feathers
I fettered was
in garden Gunnlauth's. | A forgetful heron is called,
That hovers over the ale party,
It steals men's minds;
With this bird's feathers,
I was fettered,
In Gunnlauth's garden. |

14

| | Ölr ek varð,
varð ofrölvi
at ins fróða Fjalars;

því er ölðr bazt,
at aftr of heimtir
hverr sitt geð gumi. | Drunk I became,
became over-aled
that the cunning Fjalar's;

for is ale best,
that back of gets
each his mind man. | I became drunk,
And became over aled,
At that cunning jötun Fjalar's;
Because ale is best,
That he gets back,
Each man, his mind. |

15

| | Þagalt ok hugalt
skyli þjóðans barn
ok vígdjarft vera;
glaðr ok reifr
skyli gumna hverr,
unz sinn bíðr bana. | Silent and thoughtful
should ruler's children
and brave be;
glad and cheerful
should men watch,
until his awaiting death. | Silent and thoughtful,
Should a ruler's children,
Be, and brave;
Glad and cheerful,
Should men watch,
Until their awaiting death. |

16

| | Ósnjallr maðr
hyggsk munu ey lifa, | Un-smart man
thinks will ever live, | A cowardly man,
Thinks he will live forever, |

Hávamál (The Sayings of the High One)

Old Norse	Literal	English
ef hann við víg varask;	if he with killing avoids;	If he avoids the fight;
en elli gefr	but age gives	But his age gives,
hánum engi frið,	him no peace,	Him no peace,
þótt hánum geirar gefi.	though he spears give.	Though spears may save his life.

17

Kópir afglapi	Agape fool	A fool gapes,
er til kynnis kemr,	who to kinsmen comes,	When he comes to his kinsmen,
þylsk hann um eða þrumir;	talks he about or silent;	And mutters, or is silent;
allt er senn,	all the same,	But all at once,
ef hann sylg of getr,	if he sup of gets,	If he gets a drink,
uppi er þá geð guma.	up is then mind man's.	Is a mans mind shown.

18

Sá einn veit	So one knows	He alone knows,
er víða ratar	has widely roamed	Who has roamed,
ok hefr fjölð of farit,	and has many of travelled,	And has travelled widely,
hverju geði	each mind	Each mind,
stýrir gumna hverr,	steers men each,	That is steered,
sá er vitandi er vits.	so is known as wits.	So by his knowing and his wits.

19

Haldi-t maðr á keri,	Hold-not man of vessel,	Let a man hold the cup,
drekki þó at hófi mjöð,	drink though at moderation mead,	But drink the mead in moderation,
mæli þarft eða þegi,	speak as-needed or silent,	Speak as needed or be silent,
ókynnis þess	unknown this	Unknown shall be,
vár þik engi maðr,	were you none man,	Where you alone, man,
at þú gangir snemma at sofa.	that you go soon to sleep.	Soon go to sleep.

20

Gráðugr halr,	Greedy man,	A greedy man,
nema geðs viti,	taken of-mind knowing,	If he is not mindful,

Hávamál (The Sayings of the High One)

	Old Norse	Literal	English
	etr sér aldrtrega;	eats he age-hurt;	Eats to hurt his age,
	oft fær hlægis,	often goes laughter,	Laughter is often brought,
	er með horskum kemr,	when among the-wise comes,	When among the wise,
	manni heimskum magi.	men foolish stomach.	Comes a man with a foolish stomach.
21			
	Hjarðir þat vitu,	Herds that know,	Herds know,
	nær þær heim skulu,	when they home should-be,	When they should be home,
	ok ganga þá af grasi;	and go-they then from pasture;	And then they go from the pasture,
	en ósviðr maðr	but unwise man	But an unwise man,
	kann ævagi	knows never	Never knows,
	síns of mál maga.	his about matter stomach.	The measure of his stomach.
22			
	Vesall maðr	Miserable man	The miserable man,
	ok illa skapi	and ill character	And poor of character,
	hlær at hvívetna;	laughs at everything;	Laughs at everything;
	hittki hann veit,	not he knows,	For he does not know,
	er hann vita þyrfti,	which he know needs,	That which he needs to know,
	at hann er-a vamma vanr.	that he is-not faults free.	That he is not free from faults.
23			
	Ósviðr maðr	Unwise man	A foolish man,
	vakir um allar nætr	awake about all nights	Is awake all the night,
	ok hyggr at hvívetna;	and worries at everything;	And worries about everything;
	þá er móðr,	then is tired,	And then is tired,
	er at morgni kemr,	when to morning comes,	When morning comes,
	allt er víl sem var.	all is trouble as was.	And all troubles are as was.

Hávamál (The Sayings of the High One)

	Old Norse	Literal	English
24			
	Ósnotr maðr	Unwise man	An unwise man,
	hyggr sér alla vera	thinks he all to-be	Thinks that all whom to him,
	viðhlæjendr vini;	with-laughs friends;	With laughter, are friends;
	hittki hann fiðr,	not he seeks,	He does not seem,
	þótt þeir um hann fár lesi,	though they for him malice express,	Though they express malice of him,
	ef hann með snotrum sitr.	if he with the-wise sits.	When he is among the wise.
25			
	Ósnotr maðr	Unwise man	A foolish man,
	hyggr sér alla vera	thinks himself all be	Thinks all who speak fair to him,
	viðhlæjendr vini;	with-laughs friends;	With laughter, are his friends.
	þá þat finnr,	then that finds,	Then he finds,
	er at þingi kemr,	when to assembly comes,	That when the assembly comes,
	at hann á formælendr fáa.	that he has for-speakers few.	He has few who speak for him.
26			
	Ósnotr maðr	Unwise man	A foolish man,
	þykkisk allt vita,	seems all knowing,	Seems all knowing,
	ef hann á sér í vá veru;	if he is himself in difficulty being;	If he is in difficulty;
	hittki hann veit,	not he knows,	But he does not know,
	hvat hann skal við kveða,	what he shall with quote,	What he shall answer with,
	ef hans freista firar.	if he tested man.	If he is tested.
27			
	Ósnotr maðr,	Unwise man,	For the foolish man,
	er með aldir kemr,	is among elders coming,	When he has come among the others,
	þat er bazt, at hann þegi;	that is best, that he silent;	It is best that he be silent;
	engi þat veit,	none that know,	Because no one knows,
	at hann ekki kann,	that he not knows,	That he does not know,

Hávamál (The Sayings of the High One)

Old Norse	Literal	English
nema hann mæli til margt;	except he speaks to many;	Except if he speaks too much;
veit-a maðr,	wit-less man,	The witless man,
hinn er vettki veit,	he is nothing known,	Shall know nothing,
þótt hann mæli til margt.	though he speaks to many.	While he speaks too much.

28

Old Norse	Literal	English
Fróðr sá þykkisk,	Wise so appears,	One appears wise,
er fregna kann	who learning knows	Who can well question,
ok segja it sama;	and talk the same;	And talk the same,
eyvitu leyna	unknowing hiding	Nothing is hidden,
megu ýta synir,	may pressed sons,	Among the sons of men,
því er gengr um guma.	therefore are going about boast.	Because they go about boasting.

29

Old Norse	Literal	English
Ærna mælir,	Ample words,	Too many words,
sá er æva þegir,	so are never silent,	So that never is silent,
staðlausu stafi;	unstable sticks;	Unstable stuck,
hraðmælt tunga,	fast-paced tongue,	A fast paced tongue,
nema haldendr eigi,	except rather not,	If it has not,
oft sér ógótt of gelr.	often his un-good of cries.	Cries to its own harm.

30

Old Norse	Literal	English
At augabragði	Of eye-mockery	To be a laughing stock,
skal-a maðr annan hafa,	shall-not man another have,	No man shall have another,
þótt til kynnis komi;	though to kinsmen comes;	Though he comes to his kinsmen,
margr þá fróðr þykkisk,	many then wise seem,	Many men seem wise,
ef hann freginn er-at	if he questioned is-not	If they are not questioned,
ok nái hann þurrfjallr þruma.	and gets he dry-mountain silent.	And they stay dry and silent.

31

Old Norse	Literal	English
Fróðr þykkisk,	Wise thinks,	One thinks he is wise,
sá er flótta tekr,	he who extravagant takes,	Who takes extravagantly,
gestr at gest hæðinn;	guest to guest mocking;	To mocking a guest;
veit-a görla,	knowing-not doing,	But little he knows,

Hávamál (The Sayings of the High One)

	Old Norse	Literal	English
	sá er of verði glissir,	he who about meal gabbles,	Who gabbles at the feast,
	þótt hann með grömum glami.	though he with foes clash.	In the midst of his enemies.
32			
	Gumnar margir erusk gagnhollir,	Men many are friendly-going,	Many men, Who are friendly of mind,
	en at virði vrekask;	but that meal quarrel;	But quarrel at a meal;
	aldar róg	of-old slander	Of strife,
	þat mun æ vera,	that will ever be,	There will always be,
	órir gestr við gest.	other guest with guest.	When a guest mocks another quest.
33			
	Árliga verðar skyli maðr oft fáa,	Early meal should man often have,	An early meal, A man should often have,
	nema til kynnis komi:	except to kinsmen coming:	Except when he comes to his kinsmen:
	str ok snópir,	sit and mope,	Or he sits and mopes,
	lætr sem solginn sé	let as hungry so	And seems so hungry,
	ok kann fregna at fáu.	and can inquire that few.	And can be asked little.
34			
	Afhvarf mikit er til ills vinar,	Departed much is to ill friend,	Far away, Is it to a bad friend,
	þótt á brautu búi,	though to away dwelling,	Though he dwells on the way,
	en til góðs vinar liggja gagnvegir,	but to good friend lies going-way,	But to a good friend, The way lies straight,
	þótt hann sé firr farinn.	though he so far travelling.	Though it seems far to travel.
35			
	Ganga skal, skal-a gestr vera ey í einum stað;	Going shall, shall-not guest be place in one stay;	Going shall, A guest not be, Staying in one place;
	ljúfr verðr leiðr,	loved becomes loathed,	The loved become loathed,
	ef lengi sitr	if long sitting	If sitting long,

Hávamál (The Sayings of the High One)

Old Norse	Literal	English
annars fletjum á.	another's benches about.	About another's benches.

36

Old Norse	Literal	English
Bú er betra,	Dwelling is better,	One's dwelling is better,
þótt lítit sé,	though little so,	Even though he has little,
halr er heima hverr;	master at home each;	Each man is a master at home,
þótt tvær geitr eigi	though two goats owned	Though he owns two goats,
ok taugreftan sal,	and thatched hall,	And a thatched hall,
þat er þó betra en bæn.	that is though better than begging.	It is better than going begging.

37

Old Norse	Literal	English
Bú er betra,	Dwelling is better,	One's dwelling is better,
þótt lítit sé,	though little so,	Even though he has little,
halr er heima hverr;	master at home each;	Each man is a master at home,
blóðugt er hjarta,	bleeding is heart,	Bleeding is the heart,
þeim er biðja skal	they who ask shall	Of those who shall ask for,
sér í mál hvert matar.	he this matter which food.	His food at every meal.

38

Old Norse	Literal	English
Vápnum sínum	Weapons his	His weapons,
skal-a maðr velli á	shall-not man plains about	Shall not, in the fields,
feti ganga framar,	foot going from,	Go a foot from,
því at óvíst er at vita,	for it uncertain is to know,	For it is uncertain to know,
nær verðr á vegum úti	when becomes the way about	When they way about comes,
geirs of þörf guma.	spear of needs man.	A man to need a spear.

39

Old Norse	Literal	English
Fannk-a ek mildan mann	Found-not I generous man	I have not found a generous man,
eða svá matar góðan,	or so feeding goodness,	Or so generous with food,
at væri-t þiggja þegit,	that wouldn't to-receive be-silent,	That would not be silent to receive,
eða síns féar	of his wealth	Of his wealth,
svági [glöggvan],	giving stingy,	Given stingy

Hávamál (The Sayings of the High One)

	Old Norse	Literal	English
	at leið sé laun, ef þægi.	that the-way be rewards, if receives.	That he willed a reward, if he could receive.
40			
	Féar síns,	Wealth his,	His wealth,
	er fengit hefr,	if got has,	If he gas got it,
	skyli-t maðr þörf þola;	shouldn't man need endure;	No man should endure need;
	oft sparir leiðum,	often spares disliked,	Often spared for the foe,
	þats hefr ljúfum hugat;	that has loved thought;	What was meant for the friend,
	margt gengr verr en varir.	many goes worse than aware.	For much goes worse than expected.
41			
	Vápnum ok váðum	Weapons and vestments	Weapons and garments,
	skulu vinir gleðjask;	shall friends gladden;	Shall gladden friends,
	þat er á sjalfum sýnst;	that are in themselves seemed;	As each for himself can seem;
	viðrgefendr ok endrgefendr	worth-givers and receivers-of-gifts	Givers and receivers of gifts,
	erusk lengst vinir,	are longest friends,	Are longest friends,
	ef þat bíðr at verða vel.	if that abides to become well.	If it abides that all goes well.
42			
	Vin sínum	Friend his	To his friends,
	skal maðr vinr vera	shall man friend be	A man should be a friend,
	ok gjalda gjöf við gjöf;	and pay gift with gift;	And repay a gift with a gift;
	hlátr við hlátri	laughter with laughter	Laughter with laughter,
	skyli hölðar taka	should hold take	Should they hold to take,
	en lausung við lygi.	but falseness with lie.	But falseness with a lie.
43			
	Vin sínum	Friend his	To his friends,
	skal maðr vinr vera,	shall man friend be,	A man should be a friend,
	þeim ok þess vin;	they also this friend;	To him and also his friend;
	en óvinar síns	but not-friends theirs	But enemies theirs,
	skyli engi maðr	should no-one man	Should no man,

Hávamál (The Sayings of the High One)

Old Norse	Literal	English
vinar vinr vera.	of-friend friend be.	Be a friend.

44

Old Norse	Literal	English
Veiztu, ef þú vin átt,	Know-you, if you friend have,	Know, if you have a friend,
þann er þú vel trúir,	that which you well trust,	That you trust well,
ok vill þú af hánum gótt geta,	and will you of him good get,	And will that he gets good,
geði skaltu við þann blanda	mind shall-you with him blend	Share your mind with him,
ok gjöfum skipta,	and gifts exchange,	And exchange gifts,
fara at finna oft.	travel to find often.	And travel to find him often.

45

Old Norse	Literal	English
Ef þú átt annan,	If you have another,	If you have another,
þanns þú illa trúir,	of you ill trust,	Who you trust badly,
vildu af hánum þó gótt geta,	will of him though good get,	But you will good of him,
fagrt skaltu við þann mæla	fair shall-you with him speak	Speak with him fairly,
en flátt hyggja	but craftily think	But think craftily,
ok gjalda lausung við lygi.	and reward falseness with lie.	And reward falseness with a lie.

46

Old Norse	Literal	English
Það er enn of þann er þú illa trúir	This is but about that-one who you ill trust	It is this one then, Who you trust badly,
ok þér er grunr at hans geði,	and you have suspicion about his character,	And you have suspicion about his character,
hlæja skaltu við þeim	laugh shall-you with them	You shall laugh with them,
ok um hug mæla;	and contrary-to thoughts speak;	And speak contrary to your thoughts,
glík skulu gjöld gjöfum.	like shall payment gifts.	Repay a gift with a similar gift.

47

Old Norse	Literal	English
Ungr var ek forðum,	Young was I once,	I was young once,
fór ek einn saman,	travelled I alone together,	I travelled alone,
þá varð ek villr vega;	then went I wild ways;	Then I went wild ways,
auðigr þóttumk,	rich seemed,	It seemed rich,

Hávamál (The Sayings of the High One)

	Old Norse	Literal	English
	er ek annan fann, maðr er manns gaman.	when I another found, man as man's delight.	When I found another, May is the joy of man.
48	Mildir, fræknir menn bazt lifa, sjaldan sút ala; en ósnjallr maðr uggir hotvetna, sýtir æ glöggr við gjöfum.	Mild, brave men best live, seldom sorrow feed; but un-smart man dreads everything, laments ever cheap with gifts.	Mild, and brave, The best men live, Seldom feed on sorrow; But an unwise man, Who dreads everything, And laments with giving cheap gifts.
49	Váðir mínar gaf ek velli at tveim trémönnum; rekkar þat þóttusk, er þeir rift höfðu; neiss er nökkviðr halr.	Vestments mine gave I fields in two wooden-men; warriors that seemed, when they cloaks had; naught is naked man.	My clothes, I gave away in a field, To two wooden men, That seemed like warriors, When they had cloaks, But the naked man is nothing.
50	Hrörnar þöll, sú er stendr þorpi á, hlýr-at henni börkr né barr; svá er maðr, sá er manngi ann. Hvat skal hann lengi lifa?	Withered unsheltered, so is standing tree by, warmed-not to-her bark nor needles; so is man, that is none loved. What shall he long live?	Withered and unsheltered, That stands on a hill, Neither bark nor needles are warmed, So is a man, That is unloved. Why shall he live long?
51	Eldi heitari brennr með illum vinum friðr fimm daga, en þá sloknar, er inn sétti kemr,	Fire hotter burns with ill friends peace five days, and then goes-out, when in sixth comes,	Fire hotter, Burning with bad friends, Peace for five days, But then it goes out, When the sixth day comes,

Hávamál (The Sayings of the High One)

	Old Norse	Literal	English
	ok versnar allr vinskapr.	and worsens all friendship.	And worsens all friendship.
52	*Mikit eitt* *skal-a manni gefa;* *oft kaupir sér í litlu lof,* *með halfum hleif* *ok með höllu keri* *fekk ek mér félaga.*	Great alone shall-not man give; often bought is a little praise, with half loaf and with tilted bowl got I me companion.	Something great, A man shall not give, A little praise is often bought, With half a loaf, And a tilted bowl, I got myself a companion.
53	*Lítilla sanda* *lítilla sæva* *lítil eru geð guma;* *því allir menn* *urðu-t jafnspakir;* *half er öld hvar.*	Little sands little seas little are minds men's; for all men became-not equally-wise; half is mankind everywhere.	Little sands, Little seas, Little are men's minds; For all men, Are not equally wise, Half wise men are everywhere.
54	*Meðalsnotr* *skyli manna hverr;* *æva til snotr sé;* *þeim er fyrða* *fegrst at lifa,* *er vel margt vitu.*	Middle-wise should-be man each; never too wise be; those let-be among-people fairest to living, who well many know.	Moderately wise, Should each man be, Never be too wise, Among those people, Those who live the fairest, Who know much and well.
55	*Meðalsnotr* *skyli manna hverr,* *æva til snotr sé;* *því at snotrs manns hjarta* *verðr sjaldan glatt,* *ef sá er alsnotr, er á.*	Middle-wise should-be man each, never too wise be; because the wise man's heart becomes seldom smoothed, if so who all-wise, is all.	Moderately wise, Should each man be, Never be too wise, Because the wise man's heart, Seldom becomes smoothed, If he is all wise who owns it.

Hávamál (The Sayings of the High One)

	Old Norse	Literal	English
56	Meðalsnotr skyli manna hverr, æva til snotr sé; örlög sín viti engi fyrir, þeim er sorgalausastr sefi.	Middle-wise should-be man each, never too wise be; fate his knowing none before, they who sorrow-losing calm.	Moderately wise, Should each man be, Never be too wise, His fate, If a man knows not beforehand, Those who sorrow-less be.
57	Brandr af brandi brenn, unz brunninn er, funi kveikisk af funa; maðr af manni verðr at máli kuðr, en til dælskr af dul.	Brand of brand burns, until burnt out, fire quickens of fire; man from man becomes of speech known, but to dullness from stillness.	Brand burns from brand, It burns, until it is burnt out, Fire is quickened by fire, Man to man, Becomes known by his speech, And the stupid by their stillness.
58	Ár skal rísa, sá er annars vill fé eða fjör hafa; sjaldan liggjandi ulfr lær of getr né sofandi maðr sigr.	Early shall rise, so as another's will wealth or life have; seldom laying wolf skin of gets nor sleeping man success.	He should rise early, Who desires to have, Another's life or wealth; Seldom does the laying wolf, Catch a skin, Nor a sleeping man success.
59	Ár skal rísa, sá er á yrkjendr fáa, ok ganga síns verka á vit; margt of dvelr, þann er um morgin sefr,	Early shall rise, he has of workers few, and going his work on with; many of delaying, then are about morning sleeping,	He should rise early, He who has few workers, And to seek work of himself, Much is delayed, Those who sleep about the morning,

Hávamál (The Sayings of the High One)

	Old Norse	Literal	English
	hálfr er auðr und hvötum.	half is wealth under willing.	To the keen, wealth is half won.
60			
	Þurra skíða ok þakinna næfra, þess kann maðr mjöt, þess viðar, er vinnask megi mál ok misseri.	Dry logs and coverings bark, this know man measure, this wood, that winning may matter and season.	Dry logs, And roof bark, A man can know the measure, The wood, That he may win, For the matter and the season.
61			
	Þveginn ok mettr ríði maðr þingi at, þótt hann sé-t væddr til vel; skúa ok bróka skammisk engi maðr né hests in heldr, þótt hann hafi-t góðan	Washed and fed rides man assembly to, though he see-not vestments too well; shoes and breeches shame no man nor horse the held, though he has-not good	Washed and fed, The man rides to the assembly, Although his garments are not too well, Shoes and breeches, Let no man be ashamed of, Nor the horse he holds, Though he has not a good one.
62			
	Snapir ok gnapir, er til sævar kemr, örn á aldinn mar; svá er maðr, er með mörgum kemr ok á formælendr fáa.	Snatching and gaping, who to sea comes, eagle about old ocean; so is man, who with many comes and out-of for-speakers gets.	Snatching and gaping, He who comes to sea, Like an eagle over the ocean. So is man, Who comes among many, And has few to speak for him.
63			
	Fregna ok segja skal fróðra hverr, sá er vill heitinn horskr;	Ask and say shall wise one, so as willed called wise;	Ask and tell, Should every wise man, Who wishes to be thought wise,

Hávamál (The Sayings of the High One)

Old Norse	Literal	English
einn vita	one knowing	Let one know,
né annarr skal,	not second shall,	But not a second,
þjóð veit, ef þrír ro.	nation knowing, if three rest.	All will know, if three.

64

Ríki sitt	Authority his	His authority,
skyli ráðsnotra	should advice-wise	Should every wise man,
hverr í hófi hafa;	each about moderation have;	Have moderation about each thing,
þá hann þat finnr,	then he that finds,	Then he who finds,
er með fræknum kemr	who among the-brave comes	When he comes among the brave,
at engi er einna hvatastr.	that not is the-only vigorous.	That he is not the only brave one.

65

-- -- -- --	-- -- -- --	-- -- -- --
orða þeira,	words theirs,	In their words,
er maðr öðrum segir	that man others says	That faith in what another man says,
oft hann gjöld of getr.	often he repaid for gets.	Often he will be repaid for.

66

Mikilsti snemma	Most early	Too early,
kom ek í marga staði,	came I to many places,	I came to many places,
en til síð í suma;	but to late to some;	But too late to some;
öl var drukkit,	ale was drunk,	Ale was drunk,
sumt var ólagat,	some were unlaid,	Some were unlaid (not ready),
sjaldan hittir leiðr í líð.	seldom hits tired to company.	The disliked seldom hits company.

67

Hér ok hvar	Here and where	Here and there,
myndi mér heim of boðit,	should I homes about invited,	Should I have been invited,
ef þyrftak at málungi mat,	if needed to meals food,	If I had needed a meal,
eða tvau lær hengi	but two meats hanging	But two meats hanging,
at ins tryggva vinar,	that the true friend,	In the house of a true friend,

Hávamál (The Sayings of the High One)

Old Norse	Literal	English
þars ek hafða eitt etit.	there I have only eaten.	Where I have only eaten one.

68

Old Norse	Literal	English
Eldr er beztr	Fire is best	Fire is best,
með ýta sonum	among towards sons	Among the sons of men,
ok sólar sýn,	and sun seen,	And the sight of the sun,
heilyndi sitt,	health long,	Health long,
ef maðr hafa náir,	if man have get,	If a man can have it,
án við löst at lifa.	without with vice to live.	Without vice to live.

69

Old Norse	Literal	English
Er-at maðr alls vesall,	Is-not man all miserable,	A man is not all miserable,
þótt hann sé illa heill;	though he so ill healthy;	Although his health may be bad,
sumr er af sonum sæll,	some are of sons happy,	One of his sons is happy,
sumr af frændum,	some of kinsmen,	Some of his kinsmen,
sumr af fé ærnu,	some of wealth plenty,	Some with plenty of wealth,
sumr af verkum vel.	some of works well.	Some from worthy work.

70

Old Norse	Literal	English
Betra er lifðum	Better is living	It is better to live,
en sé ólifðum,	than so unliving,	Than to be unliving,
ey getr kvikr kú;	ever gets living cow;	The living can ever get a cow,
eld sá ek upp brenna	fire saw I up burned	I saw fire burn up,
auðgum manni fyrir,	wealthy men before,	Wealth men before,
en úti var dauðr fyr durum.	and outside was death before doorway.	And death stood outside in front of the door.

71

Old Norse	Literal	English
Haltr ríðr hrossi,	Limping rides horse,	Those who limp can ride a horse,
hjörð rekr handar vanr,	flock drives hand without,	Those who have a hand missing can drive cattle,
daufr vegr ok dugir,	deaf fights and wins,	The deaf person is bold in battle,
blindr er betri	blind is better	Better than if he was blind,

Hávamál (The Sayings of the High One)

	Old Norse	Literal	English
	en brenndr séi,	though burned he,	Though he be burned,
	nýtr manngi nás.	benefits no-man corpse.	No man benefits from a corpse.
72			
	Sonr er betri,	Son is better,	A son is better,
	þótt sé síð of alinn	though he late of born	Though he may be born late,
	eftir genginn guma;	after gone man;	After his father is gone,
	sjaldan bautarsteinar	seldom gravestones	Gravestones seldom,
	standa brautu nær,	stand way by,	Stand by the wayside,
	nema reisi niðr at nið.	unless raise kin for kin.	Unless raised by a kinsman to a kinsman.
73			
	Tveir ro eins herjar,	Two are one's destroyers,	Two hosts are against one,
	tunga er höfuðs bani;	tongue is head's death;	The tongue is the head's death;
	er mér í heðin hvern	is for-me in coat every	As for me under every coat,
	handar væni.	hand expectation.	I expect to find a hand.
74			
	Nótt verðr feginn	Night becomes joyful	One is joyful at night,
	sá er nesti trúir,	so whose provisions true,	If one's accommodation is true,
	skammar ro skips ráar;	short are ships yards;	Short is the ship's berth;
	hverf er haustgríma;	disappearing are autumn-nights;	Fading are the autumn nights;
	fjölð of viðrir	many of weather	Many are the weather's changes,
	á fimm dögum	in five days	In five days,
	en meira á mánuði.	then more a month.	But more in a month.
75			
	Veit-a hinn,	Knowing-not he,	He that does not know,
	er vettki veit,	who nothing knows,	Who knows nothing,
	margr verðr af aurum api;	many become of riches apes;	Riches often beget apes,
	maðr er auðigr,	man is wealthy,	One man is wealthy,

Hávamál (The Sayings of the High One)

	Old Norse	Literal	English
	annar óauðigr,	another un-wealthy,	Another is not,
	skyli-t þann vítka váar.	shouldn't then blame know.	None should know blame.
76			
	Deyr fé,	Die cattle,	Cattle die,
	deyja frændr,	die kinsmen,	Kinsmen die,
	deyr sjalfr it sama,	die yourself the same,	You yourself die the same,
	en orðstírr	but fame	But fame,
	deyr aldregi,	dies never,	Never dies,
	hveim er sér góðan getr.	who has himself good got.	Who has got himself a good lot.
77			
	Deyr fé,	Die cattle,	Cattle die,
	deyja frændr,	die kinsmen,	Kinsmen die,
	deyr sjalfr it sama,	die yourself the same,	You yourself die the same,
	ek veit einn,	I know one,	I know one,
	at aldrei deyr:	that never dies:	That never dies:
	dómr um dauðan hvern.	judgement about dead each.	The judgement about each man dead.
78			
	Fullar grindr	Full stocked	Fully stocked storehouses,
	sá ek fyr Fitjungs sonum,	saw I before Fitjung's sons,	I saw before Fitjung's sons,
	nú bera þeir vánar völ;	now bear they beggar's staff;	Now they carry a beggar's staff,
	svá er auðr	so as wealth	Such is wealth,
	sem augabragð,	as eye-twinkling,	As the twinkling of an eye,
	hann er valtastr vina.	he as unstable friends.	He is an unstable friend.
79			
	Ósnotr maðr,	Unwise man,	An unwise man,
	ef eignask getr	if himself gets	If he gets for himself,
	fé eða fljóðs munuð,	money or woman's love,	Money or a woman's love,
	metnaðr hánum þróask,	pride his grows,	His pride grows,

Hávamál (The Sayings of the High One)

Old Norse	Literal	English
en mannvit aldregi, *fram gengr hann drjúgt í dul.*	but man-sense never, ahead goes he straight to folly.	But his sense does not, And he heads straight to folly.

80

Þat er þá reynt, *er þú að rúnum spyrr*	It is then tested, what you of runes ask	It is then proved, What you ask of the runes,
inum reginkunnum, *þeim er gerðu ginnregin*	the gods-known, they who made powers-gods	The gods' knowledge, That the gods made,
ok fáði fimbulþulr,	and coloured The-Great-Thyle	And Odin painted,
þá hefir hann bazt, ef hann þegir.	then holds he best, if he silent.	Then it is best if silence is held.

81

At kveldi skal dag leyfa,	At evening shall day praise,	Praise in the evening,
konu, er brennd er,	woman, when burnt is,	A women, when she is burnt,
mæki, er reyndr er,	sword, when tried is,	A sword, when it is tried,
mey, er gefin er,	maiden, when married is,	A maiden, when she is married,
ís, er yfir kemr,	ice, when across come,	Ice, when it has been crossed,
öl, er drukkit er.	ale, when drunk is.	Ale, when it has been drunk.

82

Í vindi skal við höggva, *veðri á sjó róa,* *myrkri við man spjalla,* *mörg eru dags augu;*	In wind shall wood strike, weather to sea row, darkness with lady chat, many are day's eyes;	Chop wood in the wind, Sail the sea in a breeze, Talk to a lady in darkness, For the day's eyes are many,
á skip skal skriðar orka, *en á skjöld til hlífar,*	for ship shall glide work, and for shield to cover,	Work a ship for its gliding, And a shield for its shelter,
mæki höggs, *en mey til kossa.*	sword strike, and maiden for kiss.	A sword for its striking, And a maiden for a kiss.

Hávamál (The Sayings of the High One)

	Old Norse	Literal	English

83

Við eld skal öl drekka,	By fire shall ale drink,	Drink ale by the fire,
en á ísi skríða,	about the ice crawl,	Crawl about the ice,
magran mar kaupa,	thin horse buy,	Buy a lean horse,
en mæki saurgan,	when sword tarnished,	A sword that is rusty,
heima hest feita,	home horse fatten,	Feed a horse at home,
en hund á búi.	when dog at home.	And a dog at home.

II.

84

Meyjar orðum	Maiden's words	A maiden's words,
skyli manngi trúa	should no-man trust	No man should trust,
né því, er kveðr kona,	nor as, are said woman,	Nor the words a woman says,
því at á hverfanda hvéli	for at a turning wheel	For on a turning wheel,
váru þeim hjörtu sköpuð,	were their hearts created,	Their hearts were shaped,
brigð í brjóst of lagið.	tricked in breast about laid.	And trickery laid in their breast.

85

Brestanda boga,	Creaking bow,	In a creaking bow,
brennanda loga,	burning flame,	A burning flame,
gínanda ulfi,	yawning wolf,	A yawning wolf,
galandi kráku,	chattering crow,	A chattering crow,
rýtanda svíni,	grunting swine,	A grunting swine,
rótlausum viði,	rootless tree,	A rootless tree,
vaxanda vági,	waxing wave,	A waxing wave,
vellanda katli,	boiling kettle,	A boiling kettle,

86

Fljúganda fleini,	Flying arrows,	Flying arrows,
fallandi báru,	falling waters,	Failing waters,
ísi einnættum,	ice new-formed,	Newly formed ice,
ormi hringlegnum,	serpent coiled,	A serpent coiled,
brúðar beðmálum	bride's bed-speech	A bride's bed talk,
eða brotnu sverði,	or broken sword,	Or broken sword,
bjarnar leiki	bear's play	A bear's play,

Hávamál (The Sayings of the High One)

	Old Norse	Literal	English
	eða barni konungs.	or child king's.	Or a king's child.
87			
	Sjúkum kalfi,	Sick calf,	A sick calf,
	sjalfráða þræli,	self-willed thrall,	A self willed thrall,
	völu vilmæli,	witch flattering,	A flattering witch,
	val nýfelldum.	foe new-slain.	An enemy newly slain.
88			
	Akri ársánum	Field early-sown	A field sown early,
	trúi engi maðr	trust no man	Trust no man,
	né til snemma syni,	nor to early sons,	Nor to early sons,
	- veðr ræðr akri	- weather rules the-field	Weather rules the field,
	en vit syni;	and wit sons;	And the wit of sons,
	hætt er þeira hvárt.	ended are they each.	Are often each ended.
89			
	Bróðurbana sínum	Brother's-slayer his	A brother's slayer,
	þótt á brautu mæti,	though to away met,	Though on the high road met,
	húsi hálfbrunnu,	house half-burned,	A house half-burned,
	hesti alskjótum,	horse all-swift,	A horse all swift,
	- þá er jór ónýtr,	- then is horse no-use,	A horse is useless,
	ef einn fótr brotnar -,	if one foot broken ,	If one foot is broken,
	verði-t maðr svá tryggr	become-not man so trusting	Become not so trusting,
	at þessu trúi öllu.	that these trust all.	As to trust any of these.
90			
	Svá er friðr kvenna,	So is love women,	So is the love of women,
	þeira er flátt hyggja,	theirs are lies thoughts,	Their thoughts are lies,
	sem aki jó óbryddum	as drive horse rough-shoe	As if one drove not rough shod,
	á ísi hálum,	over ice slipperiness,	Over slippery ice,
	teitum, tvévetrum	happy, two-year-old	A happy two year old,
	ok sé tamr illa,	and so tamed ill,	And so ill tamed,
	eða í byr óðum	or in wind wild	Or in wild wind,
	beiti stjórnlausu,	boat steer-less,	A boat steerless,
	eða skyli haltr henda	or shelter limping catching	Or the lame catching,

Hávamál (The Sayings of the High One)

	Old Norse	Literal	English
	hrein í þáfjalli.	reindeer about thawed-fell.	Reindeer on slippery rocks.
91			
	Bert ek nú mæli, því at ek bæði veit, brigðr er karla hugr konum; þá vér fegrst mælum, er vér flást hyggjum: þat tælir horska hugi.	Bare I now speak, since that I both know, faithless is man mind woman; then we fair speak, when we falsely think: that deceit wisdom mind.	Barely I now speak, Since I know both, Faithless is a man's mind to a woman, When we speak fairly, When we falsely think, That deceives even the wise mind.
92			
	Fagrt skal mæla ok fé bjóða, sá er vill fljóðs ást fá, líki leyfa ins ljósa mans, sá fær, er fríar.	Fair shall speak and wealth offer, so as will woman's love have, body praise the light-mother hand-maiden, so gets, who frees.	Fairly shall he speak, And offer wealth, So as to have a woman's love, Praise the body, Of the fair maiden, He who courts her, he gets.
93			
	Ástar firna skyli engi maðr annan aldregi; oft fá á horskan, er á heimskan né fá, lostfagrir litir.	Love blame should no man another ever; often gets the wise, that of fools not gets, desire-fair glance.	Love, blame, No man should, Ever another, Often the wise get, What a fool does not get, Desire's fair glance.
94			
	Eyvitar firna er maðr annan skal, þess er um margan gengr guma; heimska ór horskum gerir hölða sonu	Not blame a man another shall, this is of many goes heed; fools out-of the-wise makes hold sons	Not to blame, Shall another man, It is the lot of many, That makes fools out of the wise, And makes the sons of men,

Hávamál (The Sayings of the High One)

	Old Norse	Literal	English
	sá inn máttki munr.	so the mighty longing.	All powerful desire.
95			
	Hugr einn þat veit,	Mind alone that knows,	The mind alone knows,
	er býr hjarta nær,	what dwells heart near,	What dwells near the heart,
	einn er hann sér of sefa;	alone that he himself of soothing;	That alone is conscious of affection,
	öng er sótt verri	none is sickness worse	No disease is worse,
	hveim snotrum manni	who the-wise men	Than the wise man,
	en sér engu at una.	than himself none at content.	That cannot be content with himself.
96			
	Þat ek þá reynda,	That I then experienced,	Then I experienced,
	er ek í reyri sat,	when I among reeds sat,	When I sat among the reeds,
	ok vættak míns munar;	and waited my delight;	And waited for my delight,
	hold ok hjarta	body and heart	Body and heart,
	var mér in horska mær;	was to-me in wise maiden;	Was mine for the wise maiden,
	þeygi ek hana at heldr hefik.	yet-not I her to hold had.	Yet I never held her.
97			
	Billings mey	Billing's daughter	Billing's daughter,
	ek fann beðjum á	I found bed about	I found on her bed,
	sólhvíta sofa;	sun-white sleeping;	Fairer than sunlight sleeping,
	jarls ynði	earl's happiness	The earl's happiness,
	þótti mér ekki vera	thought I nothing be	I thought of as nothing,
	nema við þat lík at lifa.	except with that form to live.	If without that fair form to live.
98			
	"Auk nær aftni	"Yet nearer evening	"Yet nearer evening,
	skaltu, Óðinn, koma,	shall-you, Odin, come,	Shall you, Odin, come,
	ef þú vilt þér mæla man;	if you will to-you matter bond-woman;	If you will to bond to a woman;
	allt eru ósköp,	all are no-end,	All will be unending,
	nema einir viti	except one knowing	Except one knowing,

Hávamál (The Sayings of the High One)

Old Norse	Literal	English
slíkan löst saman".	such lust together".	Such lust together".

99

Old Norse	Literal	English
Aftr ek hvarf	Away-from I disappeared	I turned away from,
ok unna þóttumk	and love thought	And thought of love,
vísum vilja frá;	knowing willed from;	And knew what I willed from,
hitt ek hugða,	found I affections,	Met I affections,
at ek hafa mynda	that I had aim	I should aim for,
geð hennar allt ok gaman.	mind hers all and joy.	All her mind and joy.

100

Old Norse	Literal	English
Svá kom ek næst,	So came I near,	So I came near,
at in nýta var	when the night was	When night it was,
vígdrótt öll of vakin	warriors all about awake	The warriors were all awake,
með brennandum ljósum	with burning lights	With burning lights,
ok bornum viði,	and bearing willow,	And bearing willow,
svá var mér vílstígr of vitaðr.	so was to-me woeful-path of known.	So I knew my path was woefully closed.

101

Old Norse	Literal	English
Auk nær morgni,	Yet nearer morning,	Yet nearer morning,
er ek var enn of kominn,	when I was still about coming,	When I was still coming about,
þá var saldrótt of sofin;	then was housefolk about sleeping;	Then the housefolk were sleeping,
grey eitt ek þá fann	dog one I then found	I found a dog,
innar góðu konu	inside good woman's	In the food woman's place,
bundit beðjum á.	bound to-bed about.	I tied him to the bed.

102

Old Norse	Literal	English
Mörg er góð mær,	Many a good maiden,	Many a fair maiden,
ef görva kannar,	if clearly known,	If clearly known,
hugbrigð við hali;	mind-fickle to tail;	Is fickle towards men,
þá ek þat reynda,	then I that proved,	I proved it well,
er it ráðspaka	when the counsel-wise	When that wise woman,
teygða ek á flærðir fljóð;	tempted I of astray woman;	I sought to lead astray;

Hávamál (The Sayings of the High One)

	Old Norse	Literal	English
	háðungar hverrar	insults whose	Whose insults,
	leitaði mér it horska man,	sought to-me the wise bond-woman,	Sought me, from the wise woman,
	ok hafða ek þess vettki vífs.	and had I this nothing wife.	And I had not won a wife.

III.

103

	Old Norse	Literal	English
	Heima glaðr gumi	Home be-glad man	At home a man should be glad,
	ok við gesti reifr,	and with guests cheerful,	And cheerful with guests,
	sviðr skal um sig vera,	wise shall about himself be,	And conduct himself wisely,
	minnigr ok málugr,	mindful and talkative,	Be mindful and talkative,
	ef hann vill margfróðr vera,	if he wills much-wise be,	If he wishes to be much wise,
	oft skal góðs geta;	often shall good get;	Often shall he get good;
	fimbulfambi heitir,	Fimbulfambi named,	He is named a simpleton,
	sá er fátt kann segja,	so is few can say,	Who can say little,
	þat er ósnotrs aðal.	that is unwise nature.	That is the nature of the unwise.

104

	Old Norse	Literal	English
	Inn aldna jötun ek sótta,	The old giant I sought,	I sought the old giant,
	nú em ek aftr of kominn:	now am I back of coming:	Now I have come back,
	fátt gat ek þegjandi þar;	few got I silence there;	I got little there with my silence;
	mörgum orðum	many words	Many words,
	mælta ek í minn frama	spoke I to my luck	I spoke to my advantage,
	í Suttungs sölum.	in Suttung's halls.	In Suttung's halls.

105

	Old Norse	Literal	English
	Gunnlöð mér of gaf	Gunnlod to-me of gave	Gunnlod gave to me,
	gullnum stóli á	golden stool of	A stool of gold,
	drykk ins dýra mjaðar;	drink the wild mead;	A drink of the wild mead;
	ill iðgjöld	ill reward	Ill reward,
	lét ek hana eftir hafa	had I her after have	Had I gave her afterwards,
	síns ins heila hugar,	hers the whole mind,	Her whole mind,
	síns ins svára sefa.	hers the answer calm.	Her soothing answers.

Hávamál (The Sayings of the High One)

	Old Norse	Literal	English

106

	Rata munn	Rati mouth	Rati's mouth,
	létumk rúms of fá	had space about have	Had made space about me,
	ok um grjót gnaga;	and about rock gnaw;	And about the rock he gnawed,
	yfir ok undir	over and under	Over and under me,
	stóðumk jötna vegir,	stood giant's ways,	Stood the giant's ways,
	svá hætta ek höfði til.	so dared I to-have for.	So I dared to have.

107

	Vel keypts litar	Well redeemed colours	In well redeemed colours,
	hefi ek vel notit,	had I well noted,	I had well noted,
	fás er fróðum vant,	few are wise wanting,	Few are the wise in need,
	því at Óðrerir	because that Othrorir	Because Othrorir,
	er nú upp kominn	is now up coming	Is now coming up,
	á alda vés jaðar.	to men's bustling earth.	To men's bustling earth.

108

	Ifi er mér á,	Doubt I me of,	It is doubtful of me,
	at ek væra enn kominn	that I realms yet come	That I would come from,
	jötna görðum ór,	giant's realm out-of,	The realm of the giants,
	ef ek Gunnlaðar né nytak,	if I Gunnlod not used,	If I had not help from Gunnlod,
	innar góðu konu,	the good woman,	The good woman,
	þeirar er lögðumk arm yfir.	there that laid arm over.	Who laid her arms over me.

109

	Ins hindra dags	The following day	The following day,
	gengu hrímþursar	went frost-giants	Went the frost giants,
	Háva ráðs at fregna	High-one counsel to learn	The High One, they hope to learn of,
	Háva höllu í;	High-one halls about;	In the High One's halls,
	at Bölverki þeir spurðu,	of Bolverk they asked,	They asked after Bolverk,
	ef hann væri með böndum kominn	if he was with bound become	If he was bound with the gods,
	eða hefði hánum Suttungr of sóit.	or had he Suttung of destroyed.	Or had Suttung destroyed him.

Hávamál (The Sayings of the High One)

	Old Norse	Literal	English
110	Baugeið Óðinn, hygg ek, at unnit hafi; hvat skal hans tryggðum trúa? Suttung svikinn hann lét sumbli frá ok grætta Gunnlöðu.	Ring-oath Odin, think I, that won had; what shall his loyalty trust? Suttung stole he had feast from and wept Gunnlod.	A ring oath, Odin, I think I had won, Who shall in his loyalty trust? Suttung stole, He had feasted from, And Gunnlod wept.

IV.

	Old Norse	Literal	English
111	Mál er at þylja þular stóli á Urðarbrunni at, sá ek ok þagðak, sá ek ok hugðak, hlýdda ek á manna mál; of rúnar heyrða ek dæma, né of ráðum þögðu Háva höllu at, Háva höllu í, heyrða ek segja svá:	Matter is it to-speak wise-man's stool about Well-of-Urd that, saw I and silent, saw I and thought, listened I to men's speech; about runes heard I deemed, not about counsel silent High-one halls at, High-one halls about, heard I said so:	It is time to speak of, The wise man's seat, The Well of Urd, I saw and was silent, I saw and thought, Listened to men's speech; I deemed that I heard about runes, Not of silent counsel, At the High One's halls, Around the High One's halls, I heard said:
112	Ráðumk þér, Loddfáfnir, en þú ráð nemir, - njóta mundu, ef þú nemr, þér munu góð, ef þú getr -: nótt þú rís-at nema á njósn séir eða þú leitir þér innan út staðar.	Counsel to-you, Loddfáfnir, that you counsel take, - enjoy would, if you take, to-you would good, if you get -: night you rise-not except about spying seek or you let to-you in outside places.	I counsel you, Loddfafnir, That you take my counsel, You would profit, if you would take, You would get good, if you get, Rise not at night time, Except seeking to spy, Or if you are to go to outside places.

Hávamál (The Sayings of the High One)

	Old Norse	Literal	English

113

	Ráðumk þér, Loddfáfnir,	Counsel to-you, Loddfáfnir,	I counsel you, Loddfafnir,
	en þú ráð nemir, -	that you counsel take, -	That you take my counsel,
	njóta mundu, ef þú nemr,	enjoy would, if you take,	You would profit, if you would take,
	þér munu góð, ef þú getr -:	to-you would good, if you get -:	You would get good, if you get,
	fjölkunnigri konu	full-knowing woman	A sorceress,
	skal-at-tu í faðmi sofa,	shall-not-you in arms sleep,	Shall you not sleep in her arms,
	svá at hon lyki þik liðum.	so that she locks your limbs.	So that she does not ensnare your limbs.

114

	Hon svá gerir,	She so does,	So shall she do,
	at þú gáir eigi	that you care not	That you care not,
	þings né þjóðans máls;	assembly not ruler's speech;	For an assembly or ruler's speech,
	mat þú vill-at	food you will-not	Food will you shun,
	né mannskis gaman,	nor human joys,	And human joys,
	ferr þú sorgafullr at sofa.	travel you sorrowful to sleep.	And travel sorrowful to sleep.

115

	Ráðumk þér, Loddfáfnir,	Counsel to-you, Loddfáfnir,	I counsel you, Loddfafnir,
	en þú ráð nemir, -	that you counsel take, -	That you take my counsel,
	njóta mundu, ef þú nemr,	enjoy would, if you take,	You would profit, if you would take,
	þér munu góð, ef þú getr -:	to-you would good, if you get -:	You would get good, if you get,
	annars konu	another's woman	Another's woman,
	teygðu þér aldregi	tempt you never	Never tempt you,
	eyrarúnu at.	ear-secrets to.	To give secrets to.

116

	Ráðumk þér, Loddfáfnir,	Counsel to-you, Loddfáfnir,	I counsel you, Loddfafnir,
	en þú ráð nemir, -	that you counsel take, -	That you take my counsel,
	njóta mundu, ef þú nemr,	enjoy would, if you take,	You would profit, if you would take,

Hávamál (The Sayings of the High One)

Old Norse	Literal	English
þér munu góð, ef þú getr -:	to-you would good, if you get -:	You would get good, if you get,
á fjalli eða firði,	about mountains or fjords,	About mountains or fjords,
ef þik fara tíðir,	if you travel a-time,	If you travel for a time,
fásktu at virði vel.	get of worth well.	Provide yourself well with food.

117

Old Norse	Literal	English
Ráðumk þér, Loddfáfnir,	Counsel to-you, Loddfáfnir,	I counsel you, Loddfafnir,
en þú ráð nemir, -	that you counsel take, -	That you take my counsel,
njóta mundu, ef þú nemr,	enjoy would, if you take,	You would profit, if you would take,
þér munu góð, ef þú getr -:	to-you would good, if you get -:	You would get good, if you get,
illan mann	evil man	An evil man,
láttu aldregi	let never	Let you never,
óhöpp at þér vita,	un-lucky that to-you know,	Tell of your bad luck,
því at af illum manni	because that of evil man	Because that evil man,
fær þú aldregi	accomplish you never	You shall never accomplish,
gjöld ins góða hugar.	reward the good thought.	Reward for good thoughts.

118

Old Norse	Literal	English
Ofarla bíta	Sharply cut	Sharply cut,
ek sá einum hal	I saw one man	I saw a man,
orð illrar konu;	words ill woman's;	By a woman's ill words,
fláráð tunga	false tongue	False tongue,
varð hánum at fjörlagi	became his of slaughter	Caused his death,
ok þeygi of sanna sök.	and yet-not about truth blame.	And there was no truth in this blame.

119

Old Norse	Literal	English
Ráðumk þér, Loddfáfnir,	Counsel to-you, Loddfáfnir,	I counsel you, Loddfafnir,
en þú ráð nemir, -	that you counsel take, -	That you take my counsel,
njóta mundu, ef þú nemr,	enjoy would, if you take,	You would profit, if you would take,
þér munu góð, ef þú getr -:	to-you would good, if you get -:	You would get good, if you get,
veistu, ef þú vin átt,	know-you, if you friend have,	Know you, if you have a friend,

Hávamál (The Sayings of the High One)

	Old Norse	Literal	English
	þann er þú vel trúir,	then that you well trust,	That you trust well,
	far þú at finna oft,	travel you to find often,	Travel to find them often,
	því at hrísi vex	for that brushwood grows	For brushwood grows,
	ok hávu grasi	and high pasture	And high pasture,
	vegr, er vættki treðr.	way, is not trodden.	Where they way is not trodden.

120

	Old Norse	Literal	English
	Ráðumk þér, Loddfáfnir,	Counsel to-you, Loddfáfnir,	I counsel you, Loddfafnir,
	en þú ráð nemir, -	that you counsel take, -	That you take my counsel,
	njóta mundu, ef þú nemr,	enjoy would, if you take,	You would profit, if you would take,
	þér munu góð, ef þú getr -:	to-you would good, if you get -:	You would get good, if you get,
	góðan mann	good man	A good man,
	teygðu þér at gamanrúnum	tempt to-you of joyful-conversation	Attract to you, with joyful conversation,
	ok nem líknargaldr,	and take healing-spells,	And take healing charms,
	meðan þú lifir.	while you live.	while you live.

121

	Old Norse	Literal	English
	Ráðumk þér, Loddfáfnir,	Counsel to-you, Loddfáfnir,	I counsel you, Loddfafnir,
	en þú ráð nemir, -	that you counsel take, -	That you take my counsel,
	njóta mundu, ef þú nemr,	enjoy would, if you take,	You would profit, if you would take,
	þér munu góð, ef þú getr -:	to-you would good, if you get -:	You would get good, if you get,
	vin þínum	friend yours	To your friend,
	ver þú aldregi	be you never	Never be,
	fyrri at flaumslitum;	before to friendship-breach;	Before to breach friendship,
	sorg etr hjarta,	sorrow eats the-heart,	Sorrow eats the heart,
	ef þú segja né náir	if you say not get	If you may not tell,
	einhverjum allan hug.	somebody-else's all thoughts.	Somebody else, all your thoughts.

122

	Old Norse	Literal	English
	Ráðumk þér, Loddfáfnir,	Counsel to-you, Loddfáfnir,	I counsel you, Loddfafnir,
	en þú ráð nemir, -	that you counsel take, -	That you take my counsel,

Hávamál (The Sayings of the High One)

	Old Norse	Literal	English
	njóta mundu, ef þú nemr,	enjoy would, if you take,	You would profit, if you would take,
	þér munu góð, ef þú getr -:	to-you would good, if you get -:	You would get good, if you get,
	orðum skipta	words exchange	Exchange words,
	þú skalt aldregi	you shall never	Never shall you,
	við ósvinna apa,	with unwise fool,	With an unwise fool.
123			
	Því at af illum manni	Because that of evil man	Because that evil man,
	mundu aldregi	would never	Would never,
	góðs laun of geta,	good repayment of get,	Give good repayment,
	en góðr maðr	but good man	But a good man,
	mun þik gerva mega	will you make may	Will make you,
	líknfastan at lofi.	strong in praise.	Strong with his praise.
124			
	Sifjum er þá blandat,	Affinity is then blended,	Affinity is then blended,
	hver er segja ræðr	each who says advice	Each who gives advice,
	einum allan hug;	to-one all thoughts;	To all of one's thoughts,
	allt er betra	all is better	All is better,
	en sé brigðum at vera;	than so unreliable to be;	Than being with the unreliable;
	er-a sá vinr öðrum, er vilt eitt segir.	be-not so friend other, than will only say.	Be not the friend that will only speak fair.
125			
	Ráðumk, þér Loddfáfnir,	Counsel, to-you Loddfáfnir,	I counsel you, Loddfafnir,
	en þú ráð nemir, -	that you counsel take, -	That you take my counsel,
	njóta mundu, ef þú nemr,	enjoy would, if you take,	You would profit, if you would take,
	þér munu góð, ef þú getr -:	to-you would good, if you get -:	You would get good, if you get,
	þrimr orðum senna	three words chatter	Even in three words,
	skal-at-tu þér við verra mann	shall-not-you to-you with worse man	Do not quarrel with a worse man,
	oft inn betri bilar,	often the better downed,	Often the better is laid low,
	þá er inn verri vegr.	then is the worse way.	By the worse when he strikes.

Hávamál (The Sayings of the High One)

	Old Norse	Literal	English

126

Old Norse	Literal	English
Ráðumk þér, Loddfáfnir,	Counsel to-you, Loddfáfnir,	I counsel you, Loddfafnir,
en þú ráð nemir, -	that you counsel take, -	That you take my counsel,
njóta mundu, ef þú nemr,	enjoy would, if you take,	You would profit, if you would take,
þér munu góð, ef þú getr -:	to-you would good, if you get -:	You would get good, if you get,
skósmiðr þú verir	shoesmith you be	Be not a shoesmith,
né skeftismiðr,	nor shaftmaker,	Or a shaft maker,
nema þú sjalfum þér séir:	except you yourself to-you seek:	Except for yourself,
skór er skapaðr illa	shoe is crafted badly	For if the shoe is crafted badly,
eða skaft sé rangt,	or shaft seen wrong,	Or the shaft seen wrong,
þá er þér böls beðit.	then that to-you affliction bid.	Then to you a curse is bid.

127

Old Norse	Literal	English
Ráðumk þér, Loddfáfnir,	Counsel to-you, Loddfáfnir,	I counsel you, Loddfafnir,
en þú ráð nemir, -	that you counsel take, -	That you take my counsel,
njóta mundu, ef þú nemr,	enjoy would, if you take,	You would profit, if you would take,
þér munu góð, ef þú getr -:	to-you would good, if you get -:	You would get good, if you get,
hvars þú böl kannt,	where you affliction know,	Where you see affliction,
kveð þú þér bölvi at	greet you to-you affliction of	Greet this affliction as your own,
ok gef-at þínum fjándum frið.	and give-not your enemy peace.	And give your enemies no peace.

128

Old Norse	Literal	English
Ráðumk þér, Loddfáfnir,	Counsel to-you, Loddfáfnir,	I counsel you, Loddfafnir,
en þú ráð nemir, -	that you counsel take, -	That you take my counsel,
njóta mundu, ef þú nemr,	enjoy would, if you take,	You would profit, if you would take,
þér munu góð, ef þú getr -:	to-you would good, if you get -:	You would get good, if you get,
illu feginn	evil joyful	Rejoicing of evil,
ver þú aldregi,	be you never,	Never be,
en lát þér at góðu getit.	but let to-you then good get.	But let good give you good.

Hávamál (The Sayings of the High One)

	Old Norse	Literal	English

129

	Old Norse	Literal	English
	Ráðumk þér, Loddfáfnir,	Counsel to-you, Loddfáfnir,	I counsel you, Loddfafnir,
	en þú ráð nemir, -	that you counsel take, -	That you take my counsel,
	njóta mundu, ef þú nemr,	enjoy would, if you take,	You would profit, if you would take,
	þér munu góð, ef þú getr -:	to-you would good, if you get -:	You would get good, if you get,
	upp líta	up look	Look up,
	skal-at-tu í orrustu,	shall-not-you in battle,	Shall you not in battle,
	- gjalti glíkir	- to-beasts alike	When men are like beasts,
	verða gumna synir, -	become men's sons, -	Men's sons become,
	síðr þitt of heilli halir.	heathens you too enchant high.	Lest heathens bewitch your wits.

130

	Old Norse	Literal	English
	Ráðumk þér, Loddfáfnir,	Counsel to-you, Loddfáfnir,	I counsel you, Loddfafnir,
	en þú ráð nemir, -	that you counsel take, -	That you take my counsel,
	njóta mundu, ef þú nemr,	enjoy would, if you take,	You would profit, if you would take,
	þér munu góð, ef þú getr -:	to-you would good, if you get -:	You would get good, if you get,
	ef þú vilt þér góða konu	if you will to-you good woman	If you wish to have a good woman,
	kveðja at gamanrúnum	greet to joyful-conversation	Greet with joyful conversation,
	ok fá fögnuð af,	and get joy of,	And fairness get,
	fögru skaltu heita	fair shall called	For fairness shall be called,
	ok láta fast vera;	and have close be;	And have it close;
	leiðisk manngi gótt, ef getr.	loath none good, if got.	No one loathes good, if it can be got.

131

	Old Norse	Literal	English
	Ráðumk þér, Loddfáfnir,	Counsel to-you, Loddfáfnir,	I counsel you, Loddfafnir,
	en þú ráð nemir, -	that you counsel take, -	That you take my counsel,
	njóta mundu, ef þú nemr,	enjoy would, if you take,	You would profit, if you would take,
	þér munu góð, ef þú getr -:	to-you would good, if you get -:	You would get good, if you get,

Hávamál (The Sayings of the High One)

Old Norse	Literal	English
varan bið ek þik vera	wary bid I you be	I bid you be wary,
ok eigi ofvaran;	and none too-wary;	And not too wary,
ver þú við öl varastr	be you with ale wariest	Be wariest with ale,
ok við annars konu	and with another's woman	And with another's woman,
ok við þat it þriðja,	and with that the third,	And with that the third,
at þjófar né leiki.	that thieves not play-trickery.	That thieves do not play trickery.

132

Old Norse	Literal	English
Ráðumk þér, Loddfáfnir,	Counsel to-you, Loddfáfnir,	I counsel you, Loddfafnir,
en þú ráð nemir, -	that you counsel take, -	That you take my counsel,
njóta mundu, ef þú nemr,	enjoy would, if you take,	You would profit, if you would take,
þér munu góð, ef þú getr -:	to-you would good, if you get -:	You would get good, if you get,
at háði né hlátri	to hold not laughter	Do not hold to laughter,
hafðu aldregi	have never	Have never,
gest né ganganda.	guest or wayfarer.	A guest or a wayfarer.

133

Old Norse	Literal	English
Oft vitu ógörla,	Often know unsurely,	Often it is not sure,
þeir er sitja inni fyrir,	they who sit in before,	They who sit before,
hvers þeir ro kyns, er koma;	whose they rest wonder, are come;	What kind of, that has come,
er-at maðr svá góðr	is-not man so good	No man is so good,
at galli né fylgi,	that fault not follows,	That no faults attend,
né svá illr, at einugi dugi.	nor so ill, that none good.	Nor so bad, that is good for nothing.

134

Old Norse	Literal	English
Ráðumk þér, Loddfáfnir,	Counsel to-you, Loddfáfnir,	I counsel you, Loddfafnir,
en þú ráð nemir, -	that you counsel take, -	That you take my counsel,
njóta mundu, ef þú nemr,	enjoy would, if you take,	You would profit, if you would take,
þér munu góð, ef þú getr -:	to-you would good, if you get -:	You would get good, if you get,
at hárum þul	the grey-haired sage	The grey haired sage,
hlæ þú aldregi,	laugh you never,	Never laugh at,

Hávamál (The Sayings of the High One)

Old Norse	Literal	English
oft er gótt, þat er gamlir kveða;	often is good, that is old greeted;	Often it is good, that is greeted with age,
oft ór skörpum belg	often from sharp skin	Often from his sharp skin,
skilin orð koma	wise words come	Wise words come,
þeim er hangir með hám	they who hang with skins	From those who hang with the skins,
ok skollir með skrám	and fox with skins	And with the fox skins,
ok váfir með vílmögum.	and wavering among bondsmen.	And wavering among bondsmen.

135

Old Norse	Literal	English
Ráðumk þér, Loddfáfnir,	Counsel to-you, Loddfáfnir,	I counsel you, Loddfafnir,
en þú ráð nemir, -	that you counsel take, -	That you take my counsel,
njóta mundu, ef þú nemr,	enjoy would, if you take,	You would profit, if you would take,
þér munu góð, ef þú getr -:	to-you would good, if you get -:	You would get good, if you get,
gest þú né geyja	guest you not bark-at	Do not bark at guests,
né á grind hrekir;	nor from gates drive;	Nor drive from the gates,
get þú váluðum vel.	do you choose well.	Do you worthy and well.

136

Old Norse	Literal	English
Rammt er þat tré,	Strong is the beam,	Strong is the beam,
er ríða skal	that raise shall	That is raised,
öllum at upploki;	all to unlock;	To unlock all,
baug þú gef,	ring you give,	Give it a ring,
eða þat biðja mun	or that invite spirit	Or invite that spirit,
þér læs hvers á liðu.	to-you ill-will which of company.	Or grim would be the wish from company.

137

Old Norse	Literal	English
Ráðumk þér, Loddfáfnir,	Counsel to-you, Loddfáfnir,	I counsel you, Loddfafnir,
en þú ráð nemir, -	that you counsel take, -	That you take my counsel,
njóta mundu, ef þú nemr,	enjoy would, if you take,	You would profit, if you would take,
þér munu góð, ef þú getr -:	to-you would good, if you get -:	You would get good, if you get,
hvars þú öl drekkir,	when you ale drink,	When you drink ale,
kjós þér jarðar megin,	call-upon you earth's might,	Call upon the earth's might,

Hávamál (The Sayings of the High One)

Old Norse	Literal	English
því at jörð tekr við ölðri,	because the earth takes with of-ale,	For it is the earth that drinks the floods,
en eldr við sóttum,	but fire with sickness,	But fire with sickness,
eik við abbindi,	oak with binding,	Oak with binding,
ax við fjölkynngi,	corn with witchcraft,	Corn with witchcraft,
höll við hýrógi,	hall with household-strife,	A hall for domestic strife,
- heiftum skal mána kveðja, -	- heats shall moon greet, -	Heats shall the moon greet.
beiti við bitsóttum,	pasture with bite-sickness,	Pasture bite with sickness,
en við bölvi rúnar,	but with curse runes,	And runes the cursed,
fold skal við flóði taka.	ground shall with flood take.	The ground shall take the flood.

V.

138

Old Norse	Literal	English
Veit ek, at ek hekk	Know I, that I hung	I know that I hung,
vindga meiði á	windy pole about	On the windy tree,
nætr allar níu,	nights all nine,	For all of nine nights,
geiri undaðr	spear wounded	Wounded with a spear,
ok gefinn Óðni,	and gave Odin,	And gave Odin,
sjalfr sjalfum mér,	self myself to-me,	Me, myself to.
á þeim meiði,	on that pole,	On that tree,
er manngi veit	which no-one knows	Which no one knows,
hvers af rótum renn.	which of roots run.	Where the roots run.

139

Old Norse	Literal	English
Við hleifi mik sældu	With loaf me comfort	With a loaf my comfort,
né við hornigi;	nor with drinking-horn;	Nor with a drinking horn;
nýsta ek niðr,	peered I down,	I peered down,
nam ek upp rúnar,	took I up runes,	I took up runes,
æpandi nam,	loudly took,	Loudly learnt,
fell ek aftr þaðan.	fell I back from-there.	Then I fell back from there.

140

Old Norse	Literal	English
Fimbulljóð níu	Mighty-songs nine	Nine mighty songs,
nam ek af inum frægja syni	took I of in famous son	I learned from the famous son,
Bölþorns, Bestlu föður,	Bolthorn, Bestla's father,	Bolthorn, Bestla's father,

Hávamál (The Sayings of the High One)

Old Norse	Literal	English
ok ek drykk of gat ins dýra mjaðar, ausinn Óðreri.	and I draught of got the dear mead, poured Othrorir.	And I got a draught of, The dear mead, That Othrorir poured.

141

Old Norse	Literal	English
Þá nam ek frævask ok fróðr vera ok vaxa ok vel hafask, orð mér af orði orðs leitaði, verk mér af verki verks leitaði.	Then took I seeds and wisdom was and grew and well had, words to-me of words words sought, work to-me of work works sought.	Then I took seeds, And wisdom was, I grew well and had, Each word led me to other words, Words sought, Each deed let me to other deeds, Deeds sought.

142

Old Norse	Literal	English
Rúnar munt þú finna ok ráðna stafi, mjök stóra stafi, mjök stinna stafi, er fáði fimbulþulr ok gerðu ginnregin ok reist hroftr rögna.	Runes shall you find and meaningful staves, much great staves, much stiff staves, that painted The-Great-Thyle and made powers-gods and raised Hroptr gods.	You shall find runes, And meaningful staves, Much great staves, Much stiff staves, That were painted by Odin, And made of the gods powers, And Hroptr raised the gods.

143

Old Norse	Literal	English
Óðinn með ásum, en fyr alfum Dáinn, Dvalinn ok dvergum fyrir, Ásviðr jötnum fyrir, ek reist sjalfr sumar.	Odin with Aesir, and before elves entranced, Dwelled and dwarves for, Ásviðr giants for, I raised myself some.	Odin with Aesir, And before the elves entranced, Dwarves dwelled for, Ásviðr the giant before, I raised myself some.

144

Old Norse	Literal	English
Veistu, hvé rísta skal? Veistu, hvé ráða skal?	Know-you, how-to raise shall? Know-you, how-to advise shall?	Do you know how to raise? Do you know how to advise?

Hávamál (The Sayings of the High One)

Old Norse	Literal	English
Veistu, hvé fáa skal?	Know-you, how-to fetch shall?	Do you know how to fetch?
Veistu, hvé freista skal?	Know-you, how-to try shall?	Do you know how to try?
Veistu, hvé biðja skal?	Know-you, how-to ask shall?	Do you know how to ask?
Veistu, hvé blóta skal?	Know-you, how-to sacrifice shall?	Do you know how to sacrifice?
Veistu, hvé senda skal?	Know-you, how-to send shall?	Do you know how to send?
Veistu, hvé sóa skal?	Know-you, how-to use shall?	Do you know how to use?

145

Betra er óbeðit	Better is not-asked	It is better to not ask,
en sé ofblótit,	than so over-sacrificed,	Than to over-sacrifice,
ey sér til gildis gjöf;	ever to-you to gilded gift;	A gift looks for a return;
betra er ósent	better is not-sent	Better not to send,
en sé ofsóit.	than so over-used.	Than to over-use.
Svá Þundr of reist	So Thundr of raised	So Thundr raised,
fyr þjóða rök,	before people origin,	Before the origin of men,
þar hann upp of reis,	there he up of rose,	Then he rose up,
er hann aftr of kom.	who him returned of came.	He who returned after.

VI.

146

Ljóð ek þau kann,	Songs I them know,	Those songs I know,
er kann-at þjóðans kona	that knows-not ruler's wife	Which the ruler's wife knows not,
ok mannskis mögr.	and manly sons.	And sons of men,
Hjalp heitir eitt,	Help named one,	Help the first one is named,
en þat þér hjalpa mun	but that to-you help will	But that will help you,
við sökum ok sorgum	with blame and sorrow	Against blame and sorrow,
ok sútum görvöllum.	and sickness going-all.	And sickness all going.

147

Þat kann ek annat,	That know I second,	I know a second,
er þurfu ýta synir,	who need launch sons,	Who sons of men need,

Hávamál (The Sayings of the High One)

Old Norse	Literal	English
þeir er vilja læknar lifa.	they who will healer live.	They who will a healer live.

148

Old Norse	Literal	English
Það kann ek þriðja:	This know I third:	I know a third:
ef mér verðr þörf mikil	if to-me becomes need much	Of my worth is much needed,
hafts við mína heiftmögu,	bonds with mine enemies,	It binds my enemies,
eggjar ek deyfi	edges I blunt	Blade edges I blunt,
minna andskota,	mine enemies,	Of my enemies,
bíta-t þeim vápn né velir.	bite-not their weapons not staffs.	Their weapons or staffs do not bite.

149

Old Norse	Literal	English
Þat kann ek it fjórða:	That know I the fourth:	A fourth I know:
ef mér fyrðar bera	if to-me warriors bear	If to me the warriors bear,
bönd að boglimum,	binding at limbs,	Binding at the limbs,
svá ek gel,	so I crow,	So I crow,
at ek ganga má,	that I going may,	That I may go,
sprettr mér af fótum fjöturr,	spring me off feet fetters,	I spring from foot fetters,
en af höndum haft.	but off hands have.	And off hands have.

150

Old Norse	Literal	English
Þat kann ek it fimmta:	That know I the fifth:	I know a fifth:
ef ek sé af fári skotinn	if I see of villains shot	I see the shot of a villain,
flein í folki vaða,	shaft in folk rush,	A spear shaft rushing from folk,
fýgr-a hann svá stinnt,	thrown-not it so rigidly,	It flies not so rigidly,
at ek stöðvig-a-k,	that I stop-not,	That I cannot stop it,
ef ek hann sjónum of sék.	if I it sight of see.	If I have sight of it.

151

Old Norse	Literal	English
Þat kann ek it sétta:	That know I the sixth:	I know a sixth,
ef mik særir þegn	if me wounds free-man	If a free man wounds me,
á vrótum hrás viðar,	on roots raw tree,	On the roots of a raw tree,
ok þann hal	and this man	Also if this man,
er mik heifta kveðr,	that me hate greets,	Greets me with hate,
þann eta mein heldr en mik.	then eat disease rather than me.	That disease eats him rather than me.

Hávamál (The Sayings of the High One)

	Old Norse	Literal	English
152	Þat kann ek it sjaunda: ef ek sé hávan loga sal of sessmögum, brennr-at svá breitt, at ek hánum bjargig-a-k; þann kann ek galdr at gala.	That know I the seventh: if I see high flames hall about bench-mates, burns-not so broad, that I him save-I-not; this can I chant to sing.	I know a seventh: If I see high flames, About the hall of my bench mates, It will not burn so widely, That I cannot save him, If I sing this chant.
153	Þat kann ek it átta, er öllum er nytsamligt at nema: hvars hatr vex með hildings sonum þat má ek bæta brátt.	That know I the eighth, that all-among is useful-like to learn: where hate grows with war-descendents sons that may I better soon.	I know an eighth, Which all are Useful to learn: Where hatred grows, With war descendents sons, That I may soon better.
154	Þat kann ek it níunda: ef mik nauðr of stendr at bjarga fari mínu á floti, vind ek kyrri vági á ok svæfik allan sæ.	That know I the ninth: if me need about stands to save travel mine to float, wind I quiet wave about and slept all sea.	I know a ninth: If I stand in need, To save my travel to float, I quiet the wind, And the waves about, And all the sea sleeps.
155	Þat kann ek it tíunda: ef ek sé túnriður leika lofti á, ek svá vinnk, at þær villar fara sinna heimhama, sinna heimhuga.	That know I the tenth: if I see field-riders playing-tricks the-air in, I so work, that they away travel their home-skin, their home-spirit.	I know a tenth: If I see field riders, Playing tricks in the air, I work so, That they travel away, Their own forms, And their own minds.

Hávamál (The Sayings of the High One)

	Old Norse	Literal	English
156			
	Þat kann ek it ellifta:	That know I the eleventh:	I know an eleventh:
	ef ek skal til orrostu	if I shall to battle	If I shall go to battle,
	leiða langvini,	lead long-friends,	Leading long friends,
	und randir ek gel,	under round I crow,	Under the shields I crow,
	en þeir með ríki fara	but they with power travel	And they with might travel,
	heilir hildar til,	safe battle to,	Safe to battle,
	heilir hildi frá,	safe battle from,	Safe from battle,
	koma þeir heilir hvaðan.	come them safe where.	They com safely from there.
157			
	Þat kann ek it tolfta:	That know I the twelfth:	I know a twelfth:
	ef ek sé á tré uppi	if I see a tree up	If I see up on a tree,
	váfa virgilná,	waving hanging-corpse,	A hanging corpse waving,
	svá ek ríst	so I raise	So I raise,
	ok í rúnum fák,	and in runes catch,	And catch in runes,
	at sá gengr gumi	that so walks man	That so will he walk,
	ok mælir við mik.	and speaks with me.	And speak with me.
158			
	Þat kann ek it þrettánda:	That know I the thirteenth:	I know a thirteenth,
	ef ek skal þegn ungan	if I shall free-man young	If a new born free son,
	verpa vatni á,	throw water on,	Sprinkle water on,
	mun-at hann falla,	should-not he fall,	He shall not fall,
	þótt hann í folk komi,	though he among folk come,	Though he comes among folk,
	hnígr-a sá halr fyr hjörum.	sinks-not so man before swords.	And does not sink before swords of men.
159			
	Þat kann ek it fjögurtánda:	That know I the fourteenth:	I know a fourteenth:
	ef ek skal fyrða liði	if I shall among-people company	If I shall be among people's company,
	telja tíva fyrir,	tell gods before,	To tell before the gods,
	ása ok alfa	Aesir and elves	Aesir and elves,
	ek kann allra skil;	I know all understand;	I know and understand all,
	fár kann ósnotr svá.	few can un-wise so.	That few unwise can do.

Hávamál (The Sayings of the High One)

Old Norse	Literal	English

160

| Þat kann ek it fimmtánda
er gól Þjóðrerir
dvergr fyr Dellings durum:

afl gól hann ásum,

en alfum frama,
hyggju Hroftatý. | That know I the fifteenth
that howled Thjodrerir
dwarf before Dellingr's doors:

strength howled he Aesir,

but elves luck,
thought Hroptatyr. | I know a fifteenth,
Which Thjodrerir howled,
Dwarf before Dellingr's doors,

Strength he howled to the Aesir,
But luck to the elves,
Wisdom to Hroptatr. |

161

| Þat kann ek it sextánda:
ef ek vil ins svinna mans
hafa geð allt ok gaman,

hugi ek hverfi
hvítarmri konu,

ok sný ek hennar öllum sefa. | That know I the sixteenth:
if I will the wise girl
have spirit altogether and joy,

thought I turn
white-armed woman,

and change I her whole calming. | I know a sixteenth,
If I wish the wise girl,
To have together with spirit and joy,

Thoughts I turn,
Of the white armed woman,

And I change her whole mind. |

162

| Þat kann ek it sjautjánda
at mik mun seint firrask

it manunga man.
Ljóða þessa
mun þú, Loddfáfnir,
lengi vanr vera;
þó sé þér góð, ef þú getr,
nýt ef þú nemr,
þörf ef þú þiggr. | That know I the seventeenth
that me will weakly lose-sight-of
the youthful girl.
Songs these
will you, Loddfáfnir,
Long lacking be;
though see you good, if you get,
use if you take,
need if you accept. | I know a seventeenth,
That me will avoid losing sight of,
The youthful girl.
These songs,
Will you, Loddfafnir,
Which long have lacked,
Though you shall see good, if you get it,
Use if you take it,
Need if you accept it. |

163

| Þat kann ek it átjánda,
er ek æva kennik
mey né manns konu, | That know I the eighteenth,
this I never teach
girl nor man's wife, | I know an eighteenth,
This I never teach,
To a girl of a man's wife, |

Hávamál (The Sayings of the High One)

Old Norse	Literal	English
- allt er betra,	- altogether is better,	All is better
er einn of kann;	that alone of know;	That only one knows,
það fylgir ljóða lokum, -	that following songs completion, -	That the following songs completion,
nema þeiri einni,	except they alone,	Save her alone,
er mik armi verr,	who my arms worse,	Who clasps me in her arms,
eða mín systir sé.	or mine sister so.	Or is my sister.

VII.

164

Old Norse	Literal	English
Nú eru Háva mál	Now are high-one's speech	Now are the High One's sayings,
kveðin Háva höllu í,	recited high-one's hall in,	Recited in the High One's hall,
allþörf ýta sonum,	all-needed launched sons,	To the sons of men all useful,
óþörf jötna sonum;	un-needed giants' sons;	But unheeded to the giants' sons.
heill sá, er kvað,	hail so, who said,	Hail to him who spoke them,
heill sá, er kann,	hail so, who knows,	Hail to him who knows them,
njóti sá, er nam,	appreciate so, who took,	Appreciate those, who learn them,
heilir, þeirs hlýddu.	hail, they heard.	Hail to those who have heard them.

Word List *(Old Norse to English)*

Old Norse	English
', '	

A, a

Old Norse	English
abbindi	binding
að	a, and, as, as-a, at, by, for, from, in, it, of, possible, than, that, the, this, to, towards, to-you, was, were, what, which
aðal	nature
af	for, from, of, off, on, out, out-of, over, that, they, to, with
afglapi	fool, simpleton
afhvarf	departed
afl	strength
aftni	evening
aftr	away-from, back, return, returned, returning
aki	drive
akri	field, the-field
ala	feed
alda	men's, of-men's, wave
aldar	of-old
aldinn	old
aldir	elders
aldna	old
aldregi	ever, never
aldrei	never
aldrtrega	age-hurt
alfa	elves
alfum	elves
alinn	born
alla	all
allan	all, every
allar	all
allir	all, everywhere, to-all-who
allr	all
allra	all, altogether, every, everyone's, of-all, to-all
alls	all
allt	all, altogether
allþörf	all-needed
alskjótum	all-swift
alsnotr	all-wise
andskota	enemies
ann	love, loved
annan	accompany, another, each-other, next, other, others, second
annar	another, one, second
annarr	another, called-one, each, one, other, otherwise, second
annars	also, another, another's, any-other, each-other, else, other, others, others', the-other's, to-another
annat	another, any-other, another, besides, else, next, one, other, other-things, second, second-time, something-else
apa	fool
api	apes
arm	arm
armi	arms
at	a, about, as, as-to, at, back-from, but, by, for, from, had, if, in, it, man, of, on, out, than, that, the, then, therefore, this, through, to, to-be, towards, up-to, was, were, what, when, which

Word List (*Old Norse to English*)

Old Norse	English
auðgum	wealthy
auði	riches
auðigr	rich, wealthy
auðr	Aud (a name), rich, wealth
augabragð	eye-twinkling
augabragði	eye-mockery
augu	eyes
augum	eyes
auk	yet
aurum	riches
ausinn	poured, sprinkled
ax	corn

Á, á

Old Norse	English
á	a, about, all, am, and, are, a-river, as, at, at-the, be, by, for, from, had, has, have, he, in, into, is, it, of, on, on-the, onto, out, out-of, over, river, so, that, the, then, the-river, through, to, towards, upon, was, with, yet
áðr	about, after, back, before, return, returned, until
án	without
ár	early
árliga	early
ársánum	early-sown
ása	Aesir (a place, Old Norse Mythology)
ást	affection, love
ástar	love
ásum	Aesir (a place, Old Norse Mythology), the-gods
ásviðr	Asvid (a name, Old Norse Mythology)
átjánda	eighteenth
átt	descendents, direction, had, have, married, owned
átta	eight, eighth

Æ, æ

Old Norse	English
æ	ever
æðis	mood
æpandi	loudly
ærna	ample
ærnu	plenty
æva	never
ævagi	never

B, b

Old Norse	English
bæði	asked, as-well, bid-(asked), both, choose, choosing
bæn	begging, bidding
bæta	better, compensate, compensation
bana	bane, death, kill, killer, to-death
bani	bane, death
barn	child, children
barni	a-child, child
barr	needles
báru	bearing, bore, brought, carried, waters
baug	ring
baugeið	ring-oath
bautarsteinar	gravestones
bazt	best
beðit	bid, proposals, proposed-to
beðjum	bed, to-bed
beðmálum	bed-speech
beiti	boat, pasture
belg	pelts, skin
bera	bear, bore, bore-up, born, borne, bring, carried, carry, unload
berr-at	bears-not
bert	bare, uncovered

Word List (*Old Norse to English*)

Old Norse	English
bestlu	Bestla's (a name)
betra	better
betri	better
beztr	best
bið	ask, bid
biðja	ask, bid, invite, propose, propose-to
bíðr	abides, awaiting
bilar	downed
Billings	Billing's (a name)
bíta	bit, bite, cut
bíta-t	bite-not
bitsóttum	bite-sickness
bjarga	save
bjargig-a-k	save-i-not
bjarnar	Bear's (a name), Bear's (a name), Bear's (a name)
bjóða	bid, invite, invited, offer
blanda	blend
blandat	blended
blindr	blind
blóðugt	bleeding
blóta	sacrifice
boðit	bid, invitation, invited, offer
boga	bow
boglimum	limbs
böl	affliction, lair
böls	affliction
bölþorns	Bolthorn (a name, Old Norse Mythology)
bölverki	Bolverk (a name, Old Norse Mythology)
bölvi	affliction, curse
bönd	binding
böndum	bound
börkr	bark
bornum	bearing
bráðr	haste
brandi	Brand (a name)
brandr	Brand (a name)
brátt	soon
brautu	away, his-way, way
breitt	broad
brenn	burns
brenna	burn, burned, let
brennanda	burning
brennandum	burning
brennd	burnt
brenndr	burned
brennr	burns
brennr-at	burns-not
brestanda	creaking
brigð	trick, tricked
brigðr	bride
brigðum	unreliable
brjóst	breast, breat
brjóstum	breast, breasts
bróðurbana	Brother's-Slayer (a name)
bróka	breeches
bröndum	burning, firewood, sword, swords
brotnar	broken
brotnu	broken
brúðar	bride's
brunninn	burnt
bú	a-farm, dwelling, estate, farm, settlement
búi	dwelling, estate, farm, home, house, remained
bundit	bound
byr	fair-wind, wind
býr	dwells, prepared
byrði	a-bundle, burden

C, c

D, d

Old Norse	English
dælskr	dullness
dælt	easy, genteel
dæma	deem, deemed

Word List (*Old Norse to English*)

Old Norse	English
dag	day
daga	days
dags	dag's, day, day's, in-the-day
dáinn	entranced
dauðan	dead, death
dauðr	dead, death
daufr	deaf
dellings	Dellingr's (a name)
deyfi	blunt
deyja	dead, die, i-die, to-die
deyr	die, dies
dögum	days
dómr	judgement
drekka	drank, drink, drinking, drink-to
drekki	drink
drekkir	drink
drekkr	drinks
drjúgt	straight
drukkit	drank-to, drink, drunk
drykk	drank, draught, drink
dugi	could, enough, good
dugir	wins
dul	folly, secrecy
durum	doors, doorway
dvalinn	dwelled
dvelr	dwelling
dvergr	dwarf
dvergum	dwarves
dýra	animals, dear, wild

Ð, ð

E, e

Old Norse	English
eða	and, but, either, of, or
ef	as, if, maybe, of, whether
eftir	after, afterwards, along, behind, following, later, left, remained, remaining
eggjar	edges, encouraged
eiga	had, have, marriage, marry, own, owned, owning, owns, said-of
eigi	alone, did-not, no, none, no-one, not, not-be, not-of, not-to, only, owned, was-not, when
eignask	himself
eik	oak
einhverjum	somebody-else's, somebody's
einir	alone, one, only
einn	a, alone, an, one
einna	the-only
einnættum	new-formed
einni	alone, one
eins	a, alone, as, likewise, one, one's
einugi	none
einum	a, alone, any, one, to-one
eitt	a, alone, along, an, once, one, only, single
ek	i, i, i-am
ekki	no, none, not, nothing, not-to
eld	a-fire, fire
eldi	fire
eldr	fire, flame
elds	fire
elli	age
ellifta	eleventh
em	am
en	about, and, as, before, but, but-for, except, in, of, than, that, the, then, though, when, where, which, while
endrgefendr	receivers-of-gifts
endrþögu	silence

Word List (*Old Norse to English*)

Old Norse	English
engi	no, none, none-of, no-one, not, nothing
engu	none, not, nothing
enn	but, it, one, still, then, was, yet
er	a, am, am-i, and, are, as, at, be, being, but, for, had, has, have, he, i, if, in, is, is-it, it, it-is, it-was, let-be, of, of-which, out, spoke, than, that, that-was, the, then, this, to, to-be, until, was, were, what, when, where, which, while, who, whose, who-was, with
er-a	be-not, is-not, not
er-at	is-not
eru	are, are-we, is, they, are, they-were, was, we-are, were, were-they
erusk	are
eta	eat
etit	eaten
etr	eats
ey	an-island, ever, island, place
eyrarúnu	ear-secrets
eyrum	ears
eyvitar	not
eyvitu	unknowing

É, é

F, f

Old Norse	English
fá	be, few, get, get-for, gets, give, got, have, marry, pay
fáa	fetch, few, gets, have
fáði	coloured, painted
faðmi	arms
fær	accomplish, accomplished, affected, can, could, did, gets, go, goes, got
færa	be-brought, bring, brought, less, take, to-do
fagrt	beautiful, fair, fairly
fák	catch
falla	fall, fell
fallandi	falling
fann	found
fannk-a	found-not
far	go, travel
fár	few, have, malice, few
fara	faring, go, going, journey, sent, to-go, to-travel, travel, traveling, travelled, travelling, went
fari	fare, go, goes, going, passage, take, travel, travelling, went
fári	villains
farinn	travelled, travelling
farit	fare, fared, going, gone, travel, travelled, went
fás	few
fásktu	get
fast	close, fast, tightly
fátt	few, little
fáu	few
fé	cattle, fee, money, pay, wealth
féar	wealth
feginn	joyful, relieved
fegrst	fair, fairest, finest
feita	fatten
fekk	gave, got, married
félaga	companion, companions
fell	fell, mountain, slaying
fengit	caught, found, got, had

Word List (*Old Norse to English*)

Old Norse	English
ferr	away, goes, journeyed, journeys, travel, travelled, went
feti	foot
fiðr	seeks
fimbulfambi	Fimbulfambi (a name)
fimbulljóð	mighty-songs
fimbulþulr	the-great-thyle
fimm	fifty, five, give
fimmta	fifth, five
fimmtánda	fifteenth
finna	find, found, to-find, to-meet
finnr	finds
firar	man
firði	Fjords (a place)
firna	blame
firr	far, forwards, further
firrask	lose-sight-of
fitjungs	Fitjung's (a name)
fjalars	Fjalar's (a name)
fjall	mountains
fjalli	mountains
fjándum	enemy
fjöðrum	feathers
fjögurtánda	fourteenth
fjölð	many
fjölkunnigri	full-knowing
fjölkynngi	witchcraft
fjör	life
fjórða	fourth
fjörlagi	slaughter
fjötraðr	fettered
fjöturr	fetters
flærðir	astray
fláráð	false
flást	falsely
flátt	craftily, lies
flaumslitum	friendship-breach
flein	shaft
fleini	arrows
fleira	many, more, other
fleti	bench
fletjum	benches
fljóð	woman
fljóðs	woman's
fljúganda	flying
flóði	flood
floti	float
flótta	extravagant, flee
föður	father, father's
fögnuð	joy
fögru	fair
fold	ground
folk	folk
folki	folk
fór	came, comes, do, fared, forwards, journeyed, returned, travelled, travelling, went
forðum	once
formælendr	for-speakers
fótr	foot
fótum	feet
frá	apart-from, away, away-from, from, from-there, of, time
frægja	famous
fræknir	brave
fræknum	the-brave
frændr	kinsmen
frændum	kinsmen
frævask	seeds
fram	ahead, forth, forward, forwards, from, from-forward, from-going, going-forward, towards
frama	luck
framar	above, from
freginn	questioned
fregna	ask, inquire, learn, learning, news
freista	tested, try
fríar	frees
frið	peace
friðr	love, peace

Word List (*Old Norse to English*)

Old Norse	English
fróða	wise
fróðr	wisdom, wise
fróðra	wise, wise-men
fróðum	learned, wise
fugls	bird's
fullar	full
funa	fire
funi	fire
fýgr-a	thrown-not
fylgi	follow, followed, follows
fylgir	followed, following, follows
fyr	before, for, for-the
fyrða	among-people
fyrðar	warriors
fyrir	ahead, ahead-of, along, and, at, at-hand, because, because-of, because-of-a, before, before-them, before-us, by, for, foremost, for-the, from, in-front-of, present, therefore, they, to
fyrri	before, for, go-before

G, g

Old Norse	English
gætinn	wary
gaf	gave, given, was-given, were-given
gagnhollir	going-affectionate
gagnvegir	going-way
gáir	care
gala	sing
galandi	chattering
galdr	chant
galli	fault
gaman	a-game, delight, enjoyed, enjoyment, joy, joyed, joys
gamanrúnum	joyful-conversation
gamlir	old
ganga	go, going, go-they, to-come, to-go, walk, walking, went
ganganda	wayfarer
gangi	go, going, went
gangir	go
garði	garden, garden
gat	could, got, opening
gáttir	gates
geð	mind, minds, spirit
geði	character, mind
geðs	mind, of-mind
gef	give
gefa	gave, gift, give, to-give
gef-at	give-not
gefendr	givers
gefi	gave, give
gefin	be-given, given, married, marry
gefinn	be-given, gave
gefr	are-given, gave, give, given, gives, were-given
geirar	spears
geiri	spear
geirs	spear
geitr	goats
gel	crow
gelr	cries
genginn	going, gone
gengr	go, goes, going, happens, to-go, went
gengu	going, went
gerðu	did, made, make, was, went
gerir	did, does, made, makes
gerva	clearly
gest	guest
gesti	guests
gestr	guest
get	can, do, get, guess
geta	can, could, get, guess
getit	get, told-of
getr	can, get, gets, got

Word List (*Old Norse to English*)

Old Norse	English
geyja	bark-at
gildis	gilded
gínanda	yawning
ginnregin	powers-gods
gjalda	debt, expenses, pay, reward
gjalti	to-beasts
gjöf	gift
gjöfum	gifts
gjöld	payment, repaid, reward
glaðr	be-glad, glad, gladly
glami	clash
glatt	smoothed
gleðjask	gladden
glík	like
glíkir	alike
glissir	gabbles
glöggr	cheap
glöggvan	stingy
gnaga	gnaw
gnapir	gaping
góð	good
góða	good
góðan	good, goodness
góðr	a-good, good
góðs	chieftans, good
góðu	good
gól	howled
görðum	Gardar (a place), realm
görla	doing
görva	clearly
görvöllum	going-all
gótt	good
gráðugr	greedy
grætta	wept
grasi	pasture
grey	dog
grind	gates
grindr	stocked
grjót	gravel, rock
grömum	foes
grunr	suspicion
gullnum	golden
guma	boast, heed, man, man's, men's
gumi	man
gumna	men, men's
gumnar	men
gunnlaðar	Gunnlauth's (a name), Gunnlauth's (a name)
gunnlöð	Gunnlod (a name)
gunnlöðu	Gunnlod (a name)

H, h

Old Norse	English
háði	hold
háðungar	insults
hæðinn	mocking
hætt	end, ended, risked
hætta	concluded, danger, dared, end, leave, concluded, risk, the-danger
hafa	at-sea, had, has, have, have-been, having, sea, they, to-have, to-sea
hafask	had
hafða	had, have
hafðu	have, have-you
hafi	had, has, have, sea
hafi-t	has-not
haft	had, have
hafts	bonds
hal	man, man's
haldendr	rather
haldi-t	hold-not
half	half
hálfbrunnu	half-burned
hálfr	half, half-of
halfum	half
hali	tail
halir	high
halr	man, master
haltr	limp, limping
hálum	slipperiness

Word List (*Old Norse to English*)

Old Norse	English
hám	skins
hana	he, her, hers, it, she, she-is, she-was, that, to-her
handar	hand
hangir	hang
hann	called, from-him, had, he, health, he-is, held, here, he-was, him, himself, his, it, she, to-him, was
hans	he, him, his, to-him
hánum	he, him, his
hárum	grey-haired
hatr	hate
haustgríma	autumn-nights
háva	high-one, high-one
hávan	high
hávu	high
heðin	coat
hefði	had, have, had, would-have-been
hefi	had, have
hefik	had, have-i
hefir	did, had, had-it, has, did, have, have-you, holds
hefr	had, has, have
heifta	hate
heiftmögu	enemies
heiftum	heats
heila	whole
heilir	hail, safe
heilir!	hail!
heill	a-whole, hail, healthy, luck, safely, whole
heilli	enchant
heilyndi	health
heim	home, homes, households
heima	at-home, home, homes
heimhama	home-skin
heimhuga	home-spirit
heimisgarða	home-yard
heimska	fools
heimskan	fools
heimskum	foolish
heimtir	demanded, gets
heita	be-named, call, called, be-named, named
heitari	hotter
heitinn	be-called, called, named
heitir	called, called-are, is-called, named
hekk	hung
heldr	behold, held, heldr's, hold, rather, took
henda	catching
hengi	hanging
hennar	for-her, her, hers, she, to-her
henni	he, her, hers, him, she, to-her
hér	forces, here, she
herjar	destroyers
hest	horse
hesti	horse, horses
hests	horse
heyrða	heard
hildar	battle, battle
hildi	battle
hildings	war-descendents
hindra	following
hinn	he, him, in, of, the, then, this-one
hitt	encounter, find, found, it, meet, meeting, other, they
hittir	hits, met
hittki	not
hjalp	help
hjalpa	help
hjarðir	herds
hjarta	heart, the-heart
hjörð	flock, hearth, herd
hjörtu	hearts
hjörum	swords
hlæ	laugh
hlægis	laughter

Word List (*Old Norse to English*)

Old Norse	English
hlæja	laugh
hlær	laughs
hlátr	laughter
hlátri	laughter
hleif	loaf
hleifi	loaf
hlífar	cover
hljóði	hearing
hlýdda	listened
hlýddu	heard
hlýðir	listen
hlýr-at	warmed-not
hnígr-a	sinks-not
höfði	head, heads, to-have
höfðu	had, had-they, have, heads, owned
hófi	measure, moderation
höfuðs	head's
höggs	strike
höggva	break, fell, strike, striking
hold	bodies, body
hölða	hold
hölðar	hold
höll	hall
höllu	hall, halls, the-hall, tilted
hon	her, it, she
höndum	hand, handed, hands
hornigi	drinking-horn
horska	wisdom, wise
horskan	wise
horskr	wise
horskum	the-wise
hotvetna	everything
hraðmælt	fast-paced
hræsinn	boastful
hrás	raw
hrein	reindeer
hrekir	drive
hrímþursar	frost-giants
hringlegnum	coiled
hrísi	brushwood
hroftatý	Hroptatyr (a name, Old Norse Mythology)
hroftr	Hroptr (a name, Old Norse Mythology)
hrörnar	withered
hrossi	horse
hug	mind, think, thought, thoughts
hugalt	thoughtful
hugar	mind, thought
hugat	thought
hugbrigð	mind-fickle
hugða	affections, mind
hugðak	thought
hugi	mind, thought
hugr	mind, minds, thought
hund	dog
húsi	house
hvaðan	from-where, where
hvar	everywhere, where, wherever
hvarf	broke-away, disappeared
hvars	when, where
hvárt	each, either, however, if, is, whether
hvat	how, that, what, whatever
hvatastr	vigorous
hvé	how, how-to
hveim	who
hvéli	wheel
hver	each, each-of, every, how, what, who, whose
hverf	disappearing
hverfanda	turning
hverfi	turn
hverju	each, every, how
hvern	each, every, how, what, which, who, whom
hverr	each, every, every-man, one, to-each, watch, what, which, who

Word List (*Old Norse to English*)

Old Norse	English
hverrar	each, how-so, whose
hvers	each, how, what, which, whose
hvert	any, each, what, where, wherever, which
hvítarmri	white-armed
hvívetna	everything
hvötum	willing
hygg	mind, think
hyggja	observed, think, thought, thoughts
hyggjandi	thought
hyggju	thought
hyggjum	let-us-think, think
hyggr	considered, looked, think, thinks, thought, wondered, worries
hyggsk	thinks
hýrógi	household-strife

I, i

Old Norse	English
iðgjöld	reward
ifi	doubt
ill	ill
illa	a-bad, bad, badly, evil, ill, wicked, wickedly
illan	evil
illr	difficult, ill, of-ill
illrar	ill
ills	ill
illu	evil
illum	evil, ill
in	in, the
inn	a, he, in, inside, of, that, the, then, this
innan	in, inside, to, within
innar	beside, closer, inside, the
inni	in, inside, of-the, the
ins	the
inum	in, the
it	the, these, those, to

Í, í

Old Norse	English
í	a, about, all, among, as, at, by, his, i, if, in, into, is, it, lived-at, of, on, one, out, so, that, the, this, to, with
ís	ice
ísi	ice

J, j

Old Norse	English
jaðar	earth
jafnspakir	equally-wise
jarðar	earth, earth's, earth
jarls	earl, earl's, jarl, jarl's, the-earl's
jó	horse
jór	horse
jörð	earth, land, the-earth
jötna	giants', giant's
jötnum	giants
jötun	giant

K, k

Old Norse	English
kalfi	calf
kalinn	frozen
kann	can, can-it, it, know, known, knows
kannar	known
kann-at	knows-not
kannt	know
karla	man, men
katli	kettle
kaupa	bought, buy, purchase
kaupir	bought
kemr	became, came, came-to, come, comes, coming
kennik	teach

Word List (*Old Norse to English*)

Old Norse	English
keri	bowl, vessel
keypts	redeemed
kjós	call-upon
kné	allegiance, knee, knees
kom	came, come, comes, coming, had-come, went
koma	came, come, comes, coming
komi	come, comes, coming
kominn	become, becoming, came, come, come-in, coming, have-come
kona	as-a-woman, a-woman, lady, the-woman, wife, woman
konu	a-wife, a-woman, wife, woman, woman's
konum	woman, women
konungs	a-king's, king, king's, the-king, the-king's
kópir	agape
kossa	kiss
kráku	crow, crow, crow, saw
kú	cow
kuðr	known
kvað	asked, be-called, called, cried-out, said, saying, spoke
kveð	ask, greet
kveða	greeted, it-is-said, providing, quote, quoted, greeted
kveðin	recited
kveðja	a-greeting, called, greet, greeted
kveðr	called-for, greeted, greets, said, spoke
kveikisk	quickens
kveldi	evening
kvenna	woman, women
kvikr	living
kynnis	kinsmen
kyns	wonder, wondrous
kyrri	quiet

L, l

Old Norse	English
læknar	healer
lær	meats, skin
læs	ill-will
lætr	acted, allow, allowed, bellowed, had, keep, laid, lay, let, lets
lagið	laid
langvini	long-friends
lát	bellowing, have, let
láta	allow, allowed, bellowed, burn, burned, do, done, had, have, laid, lay, lay-out, leave, let, letting, lose, put
láttu	let
laun	hired, repayment, rewards
lausung	falseness
leið	a-journey, during, journey, laid, lay, pass, passed, the-way, this-way, way
leiða	lead, objection
leiðisk	lead
leiðr	loathed, tired
leiðum	disliked
leika	games, playing-tricks
leiki	game, play, played, plays, play-trickery, toyed
leitaði	sought
leitir	let
lengi	along, long, longer
lengst	long, longest
lesi	express
lét	allowed, had, laid, lay, let, lost, put
létumk	let
leyfa	allow, praise
leyna	conceal, concealing, hiding
líð	company

Word List (*Old Norse to English*)

Old Norse	English
liði	a-crew, band, company, force, forces, group, help, men, people, team
liðu	company, passed
liðum	joints
lifa	life, live, living
lifðum	living
lifir	live, lives, outlives
liggja	lay, lies, lying, the-alternative
liggjandi	laying
lík	body, form
líki	body
líknargaldr	healing-spells
líknfastan	strong
líknstafi	regard
líta	company, look
litar	colours
lítil	little
lítilla	little
litir	glance
lítit	a-little, little
litlu	a-little, little
ljóð	songs
ljóða	songs
ljósa	light-mother
ljósum	light, lights
ljúfr	loved
ljúfum	loved
loddfáfnir	Loddfáfnir (a name)
lof	praise
lofi	praise
lofti	the-air, the-sky
loga	flame, flames
lögðumk	laid
lokum	completion
löst	lust, vice
lostfagrir	desire-fair
lygi	lie
lyki	locks

M, m

Old Norse	English
má	may, may-be, tha-may
maðr	a-man, man, men, person
mæki	sword
mæla	business, matter, matters, say, speak, spoke, the-matter, to-speak
mæli	speak, speaks
mælir	speak, speaks, spoke, talking, words
mælta	spoke
mælum	speak
mær	girl, maiden, maidens
mæti	met
mætti	could, it-might, may, met, might
maga	stomach
magi	stomach
magran	thin
mál	a-meal, conversations, language, matter, matters, said, say, speech, subject, the-matter
máli	having-a-meal, matter, speak, speech, the-matter
máls	matter, speak, speech
málugr	talkative
málungi	meals
man	bond-woman, girl, man, remembered, should
mána	moon
mann	a-man, man, men, person, the-people
manna	man, man's, man's, many, men, men's, of-men, people, people's, people's, the people, the-men, the-people
manngi	no-man, none, no-one
manni	a-man, man, man's, men, person

Word List (Old Norse to English)

Old Norse	English
manns	husband, man, man's
mannskis	manly
mannvit	man-sense
mans	girl, hand-maiden
mánuði	month, months
manunga	youthful
mar	horse, ocean
marga	many
margan	many
margfróðr	much-wise
margir	many
margr	many
margt	many
mat	food
matar	feeding, food
máttki	mighty
með	about, along, among, as-well, between, it, well, while, with
meðalsnotr	middle-wise
meðan	as-long-as, long-as, meantime, meanwhile, while, with
mega	able, able-to, be, be-able, may, may-have
megi	may
megin	may, might, most, side, ways
megu	may
meiði	pole
mein	disease, harm
meira	a-more, bigger, greater, more
menn	man, many, men, people, the-men
mér	for-me, i, me, mine, more, my, myself, myself-to, of-me, to, to-me
metnaðr	pride
mettr	fed
mey	a-maiden, daughter, girl, maid, maiden
meyjar	girls, maiden, maiden's
mik	i, me, mine, my, to-me
mikil	a-great, great, large, much
mikilsti	most
mikit	great, greatly, large, many, much, very
mildan	generous
mildir	mild
mín	for-me, me, mine, my
mína	mine, my
mínar	i, mine
minn	me, mine, my
minna	less, mine
minnigr	mindful
míns	mine, my
mínu	me, mine, my
misseri	a-season, season
mjaðar	mead
mjöð	mead
mjök	many, most, much, very, many
mjöt	measure
móðr	tired
mögr	sons
mörg	many, might
morgin	morning, the-morning
morgni	morning
mörgum	many
mun	could, must, shall, should, should-be, spirit, will, would, would-be
munar	delight
mun-at	should-not
mundu	should, will, would, would-be
munn	mouth, mouths
munr	difference, longing
munt	must, shall, should, would
munu	shall, should, will, would, would-be
munuð	love, shall
mynda	aim, should
myndi	should, would
myrkri	darkness

Word List (*Old Norse to English*)

Old Norse	English	*Old Norse*	English

N, n

næfra	bark
nær	brought, by, close-to, near, nearer, nearly, near-the, when
næst	near, nearest, next, next-to, then
nætr	nights
nái	gets
náir	get
nam	took, took-land
nás	corpse
nauðr	need
né	nor, not, or, the
neiss	naught
nem	take
nema	except, take, taken, taking, took, unless
nemir	take
nemr	take, taken, took
nesti	provisions
nið	kin
niðr	descendant, down, kin
níu	nine
níunda	ninth
njósn	spying
njóta	enjoy, the-night, useful
njóti	appreciate, benefit
nökkviðr	naked
notit	noted
nótt	night, the-night
nú	not, now
nýfelldum	new-slain
nýsisk	informed
nýsta	peered
nýt	benefit, use
nýta	take-advantage, use
nytak	used
nýtr	benefits
nytsamligt	useful-like

O, o

Old Norse	English
of	about, for, of, to, too
ofarla	sharply
ofblótit	over-sacrificed
ofdrykkja	over-drinking
ofrölvi	over-aled
ofsóit	over-used
oft	often
ofvaran	too-wary
ok	also, and, as, but, of, when
orð	word, words
orða	words
orði	recited, words
orðs	words
orðstírr	fame
orðum	words
orka	work
ormi	serpent, serpent
orrostu	battle, battles
orrustu	battle

Ó, ó

Old Norse	English
óauðigr	un-wealthy
óbeðit	not-asked
óbrigðra	unfailing
óbryddum	rough-shoe
ódælla	uneasy
óðinn	Odin (a name, Old Norse Mythology), Odin (a name, Old Norse Mythology)
óðni	Odin (a name, Old Norse Mythology)
óðreri	Othrorir (a name, Old Norse Mythology)
óðrerir	Othrorir (a name, Old Norse Mythology)
óðum	wild
ógörla	unsurely

Word List (*Old Norse to English*)

Old Norse	English
ógótt	un-good
óhöpp	un-lucky
ókunnum	unknown
ókynnis	unknown
ólagat	unlaid
ólifðum	unliving
óminnishegri	forgetful-heron
ónýtr	no-use
ór	arrow, from, from-out-of, of, out, out-from, out-of, over
órir	other, others
ósent	not-sent
ósköp	no-end
ósnjallr	un-smart
ósnotr	unwise, un-wise
ósnotrs	unwise
ósviðr	unwise
ósvinna	unwise
óþörf	un-needed
óvinar	not-friends
óvinir	enemies
óvíst	uncertain

Ö, ö

öðrum	another, each, next, other, others, the-other
öl	ale
öld	age, mankind
ölðr	ale
ölðri	of-ale
ölðrum	ale-party
öll	all
öllu	all
öllum	all, all-among, whole
ölr	drunk
öls	ale
öng	none
örlög	fate
örn	eagle, eagle, the-eagle

Ǫ, ǫ

Ø, ø

Ǿ, ǿ

Œ, œ

P, p

Q, q

R, r

ráar	yards
ráð	advice, advise, advised, authority, counsel, matter, obliged, plan, plans, proposal, propose, ride, the-business
ráða	advice, advise, advised, agreed, decide, decision, discussed, plan, planned, plans, prevail, rule, to-rule
ráðna	meaningful
ráðs	advice, advise, counsel, plan, plans, solution
ráðsnotra	advice-wise
ráðspaka	counsel-wise

Word List (*Old Norse to English*)

Old Norse	English
ráðum	advice, counsel
ráðumk	counsel
ræðr	advice, discussed, ruled, rules, ruling
rammt	strong
randir	round
rangt	wrong
rata	rati
ratar	roam, roamed
reginkunnum	gods-known
reifr	cheerful
reis	rose
reisi	raise
reist	raised
rekkar	warriors
rekr	drives
renn	run
reynda	experienced, proved
reyndr	experienced, tried
reynt	experienced, tested, tried
reyri	reeds
ríða	raise, ride, riding, rode, smear
ríði	rides
ríðr	rides, rode
rift	cloaks
ríki	authority, kingdom, kingdoms, the-kingdom, the-kingdom-of
rísa	rise
rís-at	rise-not
ríst	raise
ro	are, rest
róa	row
róg	slander
rögna	gods
rök	origin
rótlausum	rootless
rótum	roots
rúms	space
rúnar	runes
rúnum	runes
rýtanda	grunting

S, s

Old Norse	English
sá	except, he, looked, saw, see, seen, so, that, the, then, this, was, was-seen, when
sæ	sea
sældu	comfort
sæll	happy
særir	wounds
sæva	seas
sævar	sea, seas
sal	hall
saldrótt	housefolk
sama	same, the-same, together
saman	together
sanda	sands
sanna	truth
sat	sat, seat
saurgan	tarnished
sé	as, be, being, he, he-be, his, is, is-being, know, saw, say, see, see-me, seen, so, this, was, which
sefa	calm, calming, soothing
sefi	calm
sefr	sleeping, slept
segir	answered, said, say, says, spoke, tell, told
segja	answer, said, said-to, say, say-of, says, say-to, talk, tell, told, to-say
séi	he
seint	late, weakly
séir	seek
sék	see

Word List (*Old Norse to English*)

Old Norse	English
sem	as, as-if, as-though, himself, how, if, it-was, me, since, so, such-as, than, that, the, then, they, was, when, where, wherever, which, as, while, who
senda	send, sent
senn	same, they
senna	talk
sér	as, as-he, for-him, he, her, hers, herself, him, himself, himself-to, his, is, one's, privately, saw, see, seeing, seen, so, that, the, their, theirs, them, themselves, these, they, this, to, to-him, to-see, to-you, with, yourself
sessmögum	bench-mates
sé-t	see-not
sétta	sixth
sétti	sixth
sextánda	sixteenth
síð	late, later
síðr	heathens, less
sifjum	affinity
sig	herself, him, himself, sign-herself, this
sigr	success, successful
sín	her, hers, him, himself, his, theirs, them, themselves, they
sinn	he, hers, his, occasion, one-day, that, the, their, theirs, then, they
sinna	hers, his, of-his, their, theirs
sinni	his, mind, once, opinion, ours, their, theirs, them, this, with
síns	hers, his, their, theirs, they
sínum	her, hers, his, their, theirs, with-his
sitja	sat, set, sit, sitting, to-sit
sitr	sat, sits, sitting
sitt	her, hers, his, long, one's, the, their, theirs, there, these, they, this
sjá	he-saw, it-seemed, looked, saw, say, see, seeing, seen, see-this, so, such, they-saw, this, to-see
sjaldan	seldom
sjalfr	himself, myself, self, yourself
sjalfráða	self-willed
sjalfum	myself, themselves, yourself
sjaunda	seven, seventh
sjautjánda	seventeenth
sjó	sea, the-sea
sjónum	sea, sight, the-sea
sjúkum	sick
skaft	shaft
skal	shall, shall-be, should, would
skal-a	shall-not
skal-at-tu	shall-not-you
skalt	shall
skaltu	shall, shall-you
skammar	shame, short
skammisk	shame
skapaðr	crafted
skapi	character, mood
skeftismiðr	shaftmaker
skíða	logs
skil	understand
skilin	wise
skip	a-ship, ship, ships, then
skips	ship, ships, ship
skipta	change, divide, divided, exchange, exchanged, of-exchange

Word List (*Old Norse to English*)

Old Norse	English
skjöld	shield, shields
skoðar	look
skoðask	look
skollir	fox
sköpuð	created
skór	shoe
skörpum	sharp
skósmiðr	shoesmith
skotinn	shot
skrám	skins
skríða	action, crawl
skriðar	glide
skúa	shoes
skulu	shall, should, should-be
skyggnast	peer
skyli	shall, shelter, should, should-be
skyli-t	shouldn't
slíkan	such
slíkt	so, such
sloknar	goes-out
snapir	snatching
snemma	early, soon
snópir	mope
snotr	wise
snotrs	wise
snotrum	the-wise
sný	change
sóa	use
sofa	sleep, sleeping
sofandi	sleeping
sofin	sleeping
sóit	destroyed
sök	blame, fault, reason
sökum	blame
sólar	sun, the-sun
solginn	hungry
sólhvíta	sun-white
sölum	halls
sona	son, sons
sonr	of, son, son-of
sonu	sons
sonum	son, sons
sorg	sorrow
sorgafullr	sorrowful
sorgalausastr	sorrow-losing
sorgum	sorrow
sótt	attended, sickness, sought
sótta	sought
sóttum	sickness
sparir	spares
spjalla	chat
sprettr	sprang, spring
spurðu	asked
spyrr	ask, asked, asks, heard, heard-of, learned
stað	land, place, places, stand, stands, stay, stood
staðar	place, places, stand
staði	parts, places
staðlausu	unstable
stafi	staves, sticks
standa	stand, standing, stay, stood, withstand
stelr	steals
stendr	standing, stands, stood
stinna	stiff
stinnt	rigidly
stjórnlausu	steer-less
stóðumk	stood
stöðvig-a-k	stop-not
stóli	stool
stóra	great
str	sit
stýrir	steer, steers, turned
sú	seen, so, that, the, their, this, was, yours
suma	some
sumar	some, summer
sumbli	feast
sumr	some
sumt	some, some-of
sút	sorrow

Word List (*Old Norse to English*)

Old Norse	English
suttung	Suttung (a name, Old Norse Mythology)
suttungr	Suttung (a name, Old Norse Mythology)
suttungs	Suttung's (a name, Old Norse Mythology)
sútum	sorrows
svá	as, so, so-as, so-did, so-much, such, that
svæfik	slept
svági	giving
svára	answer
sverði	sword, swords
sviðr	rapid, wise
svikinn	stole
svíni	swine
svinna	wise
sylg	sup
sýn	seemed, seen, show
syni	son, son-of, sons
synir	sons, sons-of
sýnst	seemed
systir	sister
sýtir	laments

T, t

Old Norse	English
tælir	deceit
taka	be-taken, take, taken, took, to-take
tamr	tamed
taugreftan	thatched
teitum	happy
tekr	take, takes, took
telja	tell
teygða	tempted
teygðu	tempt
tíðir	a-time
til	about, at, come-to, for, of, that, them, to, too, about, towards, until, way-to
tíunda	tenth
tíva	gods
tolfta	twelfth
tré	beam, beams, tree, trees, wood
treðr	trodden
trémönnum	wooden-men
trúa	believe, trust, trusted
trúi	believe, trust
trúir	believes, true, trust
tryggðum	loyalty
tryggr	trusting
tryggva	TRUE
tunga	tongue
túnriður	field-riders
tvær	two
tvau	two
tveim	two
tveir	two
tvévetrum	two-year-old

Þ, þ

Old Norse	English
þá	than, that, the, them, then, there, they, this, those, to-them, when
það	it, that, that-to, the, this, to, with
þaðan	from-there, from-there, there
þægi	receives
þær	there, therefore, they, those
þáfjalli	thawed-fell
þagalt	silent
þagðak	silent
þakinna	coverings
þann	he, him, than, that, that-one, the, then, then-one, they, this, those
þanns	of
þar	here, it, that, their, then, there, therefore, they, where
þarft	as-needed
þars	there

Word List (*Old Norse to English*)

Old Norse	English	*Old Norse*	English
þat	it, it-was, ship, so, that, that-is, that-it-is, that-which-is, the, then, there, they, this, those, to	þínum	your, yours
		þitt	you, your, yours
		þjóð	nation
		þjóða	people
		þjóðans	ruler's
þats	that	þjóðlaðar	hospitality
þau	hers, his, that, the, them, then, there, therefore, these, they, they-were, those	þjóðrerir	Thjodrerir (a name)
		þjófar	thieves
		þó	also, then, thoug, though, thought, yet
þegi	silence, silent	þögðu	silent
þegir	silent	þögull	silent
þegit	be-silent, received	þola	endure, endures
þegjandi	silence, silently	þöll	unsheltered
þegn	free-man, thane	þörf	need, needed, needs
þeim	of-them, that, the, their, theirs, them, then, these, they, those, to, to-them, were-they, with-them	þorpi	tree
		þótt	though, thought
		þótti	as-seemed, seem, seemed, think, thinks, thought, as-seemed, was-thought
þeims	he		
þeir	the, their, theirs, them, then, there, these, they, they-were, this, those, you	þóttumk	seemed, thought
		þóttusk	seemed
		þræli	thrall
þeira	are-they, of, of-them, the, their, theirs, them, there, they, this, those	þrettánda	thirteenth
		þriðja	third
		þrimr	third, three
þeirar	their, there	þrír	three
þeiri	their, there, they	þróask	grows
þeirs	they	þruma	silent
þér	then, then, they, to-you, then, to-your, you, your, yours, you-to	þrumir	hovers, silent
		þú	are-you, you, your
		þul	sage
þerru	towel	þular	wise-man's
þess	of-this, that, these, this, this-is	þundr	Thundr (a name, Old Norse Mythology)
þessa	his, these, this	þunnu	tuned
þessu	his, these, this	þurfu	need
þeygi	yet-not	þurra	dry
þiggja	accept, accepted, receive, to-receive	þurrfjallr	Dry-Mountain (a place)
þiggr	accept, accepted	þveginn	washed
þik	you, your, yours		
þingi	assembly		
þings	assembly, the-assembly		

Word List (*Old Norse to English*)

Old Norse	English
því	according, accordingly, according-to, as, because, because-of, before, for, in, of, since, that, the, then, therefore, this, what, with
þykkir	consider, considered, seemed, seems, think, thought
þykkisk	appears, seem, seems, thinks
þylja	to-speak
þylsk	talks
þyrftak	needed
þyrfti	need, needed, needs

U, u

Old Norse	English
uggir	dreads
ulfi	wolf
ulfr	wolf
um	about, about-a, among, around, as-far-as, at, contrary-to, for, from, in, inclined, of, over, regarding
una	content
und	and, under
undaðr	wounded
undir	behind, below, depended, from-beneath, from-under, near, submitted, to, under, up-to
ungan	young
ungr	a-young, young
unna	grant, love
unnit	committed, deserved, earned, spared, win, winning, won, work
unz	until
upp	above, open, to-open, up, upped, up-to-the-mountains
uppi	about, stand-up, up
upploki	unlock
urðarbrunni	Well-of-Urd (a place)
urðu-t	became-not

Ú, ú

Old Norse	English
út	back, back-from, from, out, out-from, back, out-of, outside
úti	about, out, outside

V, v

Old Norse	English
vá	difficulty, slew
váar	know
vaða	rush
váða	clothes
váðir	vestments
váðum	clothes, vestments
væddr	vestments
væni	expectation
væra	realms
væri	had, is, it-was, it-would-be, should-be, was, were, would, would-be
væri-t	wouldn't
vættak	waited
vættki	not
váfa	waving
váfir	wavering
vági	inlet, wave
vakin	awake
vakir	awake, woke
val	foe
válaðs	needy
valtastr	unstable
váluðum	choose
vamma	faults
vánar	hope
vanr	accustomed, custom, free, lacking, without

Word List (*Old Norse to English*)

Old Norse	English
vant	difficulty, missing, wanting
vápn	weapon, weapons
vápnum	weapons
var	as, as, it-was, stayed, then, there-was, was, as, were, when, where, who
vár	be, been, our, spring, sprung, were, what-was, will
varan	wary
varask	avoids
varastr	wariest
varð	became, came, there-was, was, went, were
vari	wary
varir	aware, foreseen
vark	was, when
váru	being, ours, that-was, wares, was, were, when
vatni	river, water
vatns	water
vaxa	grew, grow
vaxanda	waxing
veðr	weather, wind
veðri	weather
vega	fight, ways
vegir	way, ways
vegnest	wares
vegr	fights, slayed, way
vegr-a	carry-not
vegum	way
veistu	know-you
veit	knew, know, knowing, known, knows
veit-a	knowing-not, wit-less
veiztu	know-you
vel	a, well
velir	staffs
vellanda	boiling
velli	field, fields, plains
ver	be, were
vér	our, we, we-are
vera	be, been, being, be-it, come-to, had-been, it-be, it-was, shall-be, to-be, was, were
verða	as, be, became, become, becoming, being, to-be, was, were
verðar	meal
verði	be, became, become, meal, will-be, worth-of
verði-t	become-not
verðr	became, become, becomes, bring, was, were, worth
verir	be
verk	work
verka	work
verki	work
verks	works
verkum	actions, works
verpa	throw
verr	the-worst, worse
verra	worse, worst
verri	worse, worsen
versnar	worsens
veru	being
vés	bustling
vesall	miserable
vettki	nothing
vex	grew, grows
við	about, against, as, at, by, from, in, known, of, off, on, that, therefore, thereore, to, we, with, within, wood
víða	many, spread-in, widely
viðar	tree, wood
viðhlæjendr	with-laughs
viði	timber, tree, willow, woods
viðrgefendr	worth-givers
viðrir	weather
vífs	wife
víg	killing, killing-of

Word List (*Old Norse to English*)

Old Norse	English
vígdjarft	brave
vígdrótt	warriors
vil	will, wish
víl	trouble
vildu	wanted, will, willed, willing, would
vilja	he-willed, the-will-of, will, willed, willing, wish, wished, would
vill	wanted-to, will, willed, willed-to, willow, wills, wish, wished, wished-to, wishes, would
villar	away
vill-at	will-not
villr	wild
vilmæli	flattering
vílmögum	bondsmen
vílstígr	woeful-path
vilt	like, will, wish
vin	a-friend, friend
vina	friends
vinar	friend, of-friend
vind	wind
vindga	windy
vindi	wind
vini	friends
vinir	friends
vinnask	work
vinnk	win, work
vinr	friend
vinskapr	friendship
vinum	friends
virði	meal, valued, worth
virgilná	hanging-corpse
vísum	knowing
vit	into, knew, know, known, sense, to, we, wit, with
vita	certainly, he-knew, knew, know, knowing, to-know
vitaðr	known
vitandi	known
viti	knew, knowing

Old Norse	English
víti	misfortune
vítka	blame
vits	wits
vitu	know
völ	choice
völu	witch
vörum	to-the-wary
vrekask	quarrel
vrótum	roots

W, w

X, x

Y, y

Old Norse	English
yfir	about, across, over, up
ynði	happiness
yrkjendr	workers

Ý, ý

Old Norse	English
ýta	launch, launched, out-to, pressed, pushed, towards

Z, z

Word List *(English to Old Norse)*

English	Old Norse	English	Old Norse
		and	en, ok, ok
		another	annan, annar, annarr
		another's	annars
		answer	svára
A, a		apes	api
		appears	þykkisk
a	á, er, í	appreciate	njóti
abides	bíðr	are	er, eru, erusk, ro
about	á, at, en, í, of, til, um, úti	arm	arm
accept	þiggr	arms	armi, faðmi
accomplish	fær	around	um
across	yfir	arrows	fleini
advice	ráð, ræðr	as	er, sem, svá, því
advice-wise	ráðsnotra	ask	biðja, fregna, spyrr
advise	ráða	asked	spurðu
aesir	ása, ásum	as-needed	þarft
affections	hugða	assembly	þingi, þings
affinity	sifjum	astray	flærðir
affliction	böl, böls, bölvi	astree	ásviðr
after	eftir	at	á, að, at, er
agape	kópir	a-time	tíðir
age	elli	authority	ríki
age-hurt	aldrtrega	autumn-nights	haustgríma
ahead	fram	avoids	varask
aim	mynda	awaiting	bíðr
ale	öl, ölðr, öls	awake	vakin, vakir
ale-party	ölðrum	aware	varir
alike	glíkir	away	brautu, villar
all	á, alla, allan, allar, allir, allr, allra, alls, allt, öll, öllu, öllum	away-from	aftr
all-among	öllum		
all-needed	allþörf	**B, b**	
all-swift	alskjótum		
all-wise	alsnotr	back	aftr
alone	einn, einni, eitt	badly	illa
along	eitt, lengi	bare	bert
also	ok	bark	börkr, næfra
altogether	allt	bark-at	geyja
am	em	battle	hildar, hildi, orrostu, orrustu
among	í, með	be	sé, ver, vera, verir
among-people	fyrða		
ample	ærna		

Word List (*English to Old Norse*)

English	Old Norse	English	Old Norse
beam	*tré*	boiling	*vellanda*
bear	*bera*	bolthorn	*bölþorns*
bearing	*bornum*	bolverk	*bölverki*
bear's	*bjarnar*	bonds	*hafts*
bears-not	*berr-at*	bondsmen	*vílmögum*
became	*varð*	bond-woman	*man*
became-not	*urðu-t*	born	*alinn*
because	*því*	both	*bæði*
become	*kominn, verða, verðr*	bought	*kaupir*
become-not	*verði-t*	bound	*böndum, bundit*
becomes	*verðr*	bow	*boga*
bed	*beðjum*	bowl	*keri*
bed-speech	*beðmálum*	brand	*brandi, brandr*
before	*áðr, fyr, fyrir, fyrri, því*	brave	*fræknir, vígdjarft*
begging	*bæn*	breast	*brjóstum*
be-glad	*glaðr*	breat	*brjóst*
being	*sé, vera, veru*	breeches	*bróka*
bench	*fleti*	bride	*brigðr*
benches	*fletjum*	bride's	*brúðar*
bench-mates	*sessmögum*	broad	*breitt*
benefits	*nýtr*	broken	*brotnar, brotnu*
be-not	*er-a*	brother's-slayer	*bróðurbana*
be-silent	*þegit*	brushwood	*hrísi*
best	*bazt, beztr*	burden	*byrði*
bestla's	*bestlu*	burned	*brenna, brenndr*
better	*bæta, betra, betri*	burning	*brennanda, brennandum*
bid	*beðit, bið*		
Billing's	*Billings*	burns	*brenn, brennr*
binding	*abbindi, bönd*	burns-not	*brennr-at*
bird's	*fugls*	burnt	*brennd, brunninn*
bite-not	*bíta-t*	bustling	*vés*
bite-sickness	*bitsóttum*	but	*eða, en, enn*
blame	*firna, sök, sökum, vítka*	buy	*kaupa*
		by	*á, nær, við*
bleeding	*blóðugt*		
blend	*blanda*		
blended	*blandat*		

C, c

English	Old Norse
blind	*blindr*
blunt	*deyfi*
boast	*guma*	calf	*kalfi*
boastful	*hræsinn*	called	*heita, heitinn, heitir*
boat	*beiti*	call-upon	*kjós*
body	*hold, líki*	calm	*sefa, sefi*
		calming	*sefa*

Word List (*English to Old Norse*)

English	Old Norse	English	Old Norse
came	*kom*	cow	*kú*
can	*kann*	crafted	*skapaðr*
care	*gáir*	craftily	*flátt*
carry-not	*vegr-a*	crawl	*skríða*
catch	*fák*	creaking	*brestanda*
catching	*henda*	created	*sköpuð*
cattle	*fé*	cries	*gelr*
change	*sný*	crow	*gel, kráku*
chant	*galdr*	curse	*bölvi*
character	*geði, skapi*	cut	*bíta*
chat	*spjalla*		
chattering	*galandi*		
cheap	*glöggr*		
cheerful	*reifr*		

D, d

English	Old Norse	English	Old Norse
child	*barn, barni*	dared	*hætta*
choice	*völ*	darkness	*myrkri*
choose	*váluðum*	daughter	*mey*
clash	*glami*	day	*dag, dags*
clearly	*gerva, görva*	days	*daga, dögum*
cloaks	*rift*	day's	*dags*
close	*fast*	dead	*dauðan*
clothes	*váða*	deaf	*daufr*
coat	*heðin*	dear	*dýra*
coiled	*hringlegnum*	death	*bana, bani, dauðr*
coloured	*fáði*	deceit	*tælir*
colours	*litar*	deemed	*dæma*
come	*kemr, koma, komi, kominn*	delight	*gaman, munar*
		dellingr's	*dellings*
comes	*kemr, komi*	departed	*afhvarf*
comfort	*sældu*	desire-fair	*lostfagrir*
coming	*kemr, komi, kominn*	destroyed	*sóit*
companion	*félaga*	destroyers	*herjar*
company	*líð, liði, liðu*	die	*deyja, deyr*
completion	*lokum*	dies	*deyr*
content	*una*	difficulty	*vá*
contrary-to	*um*	disappeared	*hvarf*
corn	*ax*	disappearing	*hverf*
corpse	*nás*	disease	*mein*
counsel	*ráð, ráðs, ráðum, ráðumk*	disliked	*leiðum*
		do	*get*
counsel-wise	*ráðspaka*	does	*gerir*
cover	*hlífar*	dog	*grey, hund*
coverings	*þakinna*	doing	*görla*

Word List (*English to Old Norse*)

English	*Old Norse*	English	*Old Norse*
doors	*durum*	eleventh	*ellifta*
doorway	*durum*	elves	*alfa, alfum*
doubt	*ifi*	enchant	*heilli*
down	*niðr*	ended	*hætt*
downed	*bilar*	endure	*þola*
drank	*drykk*	enemies	*andskota, heiftmögu, óvinir*
dreads	*uggir*		
drink	*drekka, drekki, drekkir, drykk*	enemy	*fjándum*
		enjoy	*njóta*
drinking-horn	*hornigi*	entranced	*dáinn*
drinks	*drekkr*	equally-wise	*jafnspakir*
drive	*aki, hrekir*	evening	*aftni, kveldi*
drives	*rekr*	ever	*æ, aldregi, ey*
drunk	*drukkit, ölr*	every	*hvern, hverr*
dry	*þurra*	everything	*hotvetna, hvívetna*
dry-mountain	*þurrfjallr*	everywhere	*hvar*
dullness	*dælskr*	evil	*illan, illu, illum*
dwarf	*dvergr*	except	*nema*
dwarves	*dvergum*	exchange	*skipta*
dwelled	*dvalinn*	expectation	*væni*
dwelling	*bú, búi, dvelr*	experienced	*reynda*
dwells	*býr*	express	*lesi*
		extravagant	*flótta*
		eye-mockery	*augabragði*
		eyes	*augu, augum*
		eye-twinkling	*augabragð*

E, e

each	*hvárt, hver, hverju, hvern, hverr*		

F, f

English	*Old Norse*
eagle	*örn*
earl's	*jarls*
early	*ár, árliga, snemma*
early-sown	*ársánum*
ears	*eyrum*
ear-secrets	*eyrarúnu*
earth	*jaðar, jörð*
earth's	*jarðar*
easy	*dælt*
eat	*eta*
eaten	*etit*
eats	*etr*
edges	*eggjar*
eighteenth	*átjánda*
eighth	*átta*
elders	*aldir*

English	*Old Norse*
fair	*fagrt, fegrst, fögru*
fairest	*fegrst*
fall	*falla*
falling	*fallandi*
falsely	*flást*
falseness	*lausung*
fame	*orðstírr*
famous	*frægja*
far	*firr*
fared	*farit*
fast-paced	*hraðmælt*
fate	*örlög*
father	*föður*

Word List (*English to Old Norse*)

English	*Old Norse*
fatten	*feita*
fault	*galli*
faults	*vamma*
feast	*sumbli*
feathers	*fjöðrum*
fed	*mettr*
feed	*ala*
feeding	*matar*
feet	*fótum*
fell	*fell*
fetch	*fáa*
fettered	*fjötraðr*
fetters	*fjöturr*
few	*fáa, fár, fás, fátt, fátt, fáu*
field	*akri*
field-riders	*túnriður*
fields	*velli*
fifteenth	*fimmtánda*
fifth	*fimmta*
fights	*vegr*
fimbulfambi	*fimbulfambi*
find	*finna*
finds	*finnr*
fire	*eld, eldi, eldr, elds, funa, funi*
firewood	*bröndum*
fitjung's	*fitjungs*
five	*fimm*
fjalar's	*fjalars*
fjords	*firði*
flame	*loga*
flames	*loga*
flattering	*vilmæli*
float	*floti*
flock	*hjörð*
flood	*flóði*
flying	*fljúganda*
foe	*val*
foes	*grömum*
folk	*folk, folki*
following	*fylgir, hindra*
follows	*fylgi*
folly	*dul*
food	*mat, matar*
fool	*afglapi, apa*
foolish	*heimskum*
fools	*heimska, heimskan*
foot	*feti, fótr*
for	*á, at, fyrir, of, því, til, um*
forgetful-heron	*óminnishegri*
form	*lík*
for-me	*mér*
for-speakers	*formælendr*
forward	*fram*
found	*fann*
found-not	*fannk-a*
fourteenth	*fjögurtánda*
fourth	*fjórða*
fox	*skollir*
free	*vanr*
free-man	*þegn*
frees	*fríar*
friend	*vin, vinar, vinr*
friends	*vina, vini, vinir, vinum*
friendship	*vinskapr*
friendship-breach	*flaumslitum*
from	*á, af, frá, framar, ór*
from-there	*þaðan*
frost-giants	*hrímþursar*
frozen	*kalinn*
full	*fullar*
full-knowing	*fjölkunnigri*
false	*fláráð*

G, g

English	*Old Norse*
gabbles	*glissir*
gaping	*gnapir*
garden	*garði*
gates	*gáttir, grind*
gave	*gaf, gefinn*
generous	*mildan*
get	*fá, fásktu, geta, getit, getr, náir*

English	Old Norse
gets	*fá, fáa, fær, getr, heimtir, nái*
giant	*jötun*
giants	*jötnum*
giants'	*jötna*
giant's	*jötna*
gift	*gjöf*
gifts	*gjöfum*
gilded	*gildis*
girl	*man, mans, mey*
give	*gef, gefa, gefi*
give-not	*gef-at*
givers	*gefendr*
gives	*gefr*
giving	*svági*
glad	*glaðr*
gladden	*gleðjask*
glance	*litir*
glide	*skriðar*
gnaw	*gnaga*
go	*gangir*
goats	*geitr*
gods	*rögna, tíva*
gods-known	*reginkunnum*
goes	*fær, gengr*
goes-out	*sloknar*
going	*ganga, gangi, gengr*
going-affectionate	*gagnhollir*
going-all	*görvöllum*
going-way	*gagnvegir*
golden	*gullnum*
gone	*genginn*
good	*dugi, góð, góða, góðan, góðr, góðs, góðu, gótt*
goodness	*góðan*
got	*fekk, fengit, gat, getr*
go-they	*ganga*
gravestones	*bautarsteinar*
great	*mikit, stóra*
greedy	*gráðugr*
greet	*kveð, kveðja*
greeted	*kveða*

English	Old Norse
greets	*kveðr*
grew	*vaxa*
grey-haired	*hárum*
ground	*fold*
grows	*þróask, vex*
grunting	*rýtanda*
guest	*gest, gestr*
guests	*gesti*
gunnlauth's	*gunnlaðar*
gunnlod	*gunnlaðar, gunnlöð, gunnlöðu*

H, h

English	Old Norse
had	*hafa, hafask, hafða, hafi, hefði, hefi, hefik, höfðu*
hail	*heilir, heill*
hail!	*heilir!*
half	*half, hálfr, halfum*
half-burned	*hálfbrunnu*
hall	*höll, höllu, sal*
halls	*höllu, sölum*
hand	*handar*
hand-maiden	*mans*
hands	*höndum*
hang	*hangir*
hanging	*hengi*
hanging-corpse	*virgilná*
happiness	*ynði*
happy	*sæll, teitum*
has	*á, er, hefr*
has-not	*hafi-t*
haste	*bráðr*
hate	*hatr, heifta*
have	*átt, er, fá, fáa, hafa, hafða, hafðu, haft, hefr*
he	*hann, hans, hánum, hinn, sá, sé, séi, sér, þeims*
head's	*höfuðs*
healer	*læknar*
healing-spells	*líknargaldr*

Word List (*English to Old Norse*)

English	Old Norse	English	Old Norse
health	*hann, heilyndi*	howled	*gól*
healthy	*heill*	how-to	*hvé*
heard	*heyrða, hlýddu*	hroptatyr	*hroftatý*
hearing	*hljóði*	hroptr	*hroftr*
heart	*hjarta*	hung	*hekk*
hearts	*hjörtu*	hungry	*solginn*
heathens	*síðr*		
heats	*heiftum*		
heed	*guma*		
held	*heldr*		
help	*hjalp, hjalpa*		
her	*hana, hennar*		
herds	*hjarðir*		
here	*hér*		
hers	*hennar, síns*		
hiding	*leyna*		
high	*halir, hávan, hávu*		
high-one	*háva*		
high-one's	*háva*		
him	*hann, hánum, þann*		
himself	*eignask, sér, sig, sjalfr*		
his	*hans, hánum, sér, sín, sinn, sinni, síns, sínum, sitt*		
his-way	*brautu*		
hits	*hittir*		
hold	*háði, heldr, hölða, hölðar*		
hold-not	*haldi-t*		
holds	*hefir*		
home	*búi, heim, heima*		
homes	*heim*		
home-skin	*heimhama*		
home-spirit	*heimhuga*		
home-yard	*heimisgarða*		
hope	*vánar*		
horse	*hest, hesti, hests, hrossi, jó, jór, mar*		
hospitality	*þjóðlaðar*		
hotter	*heitari*		
house	*húsi*		
housefolk	*saldrótt*		
household-strife	*hýrógi*		
hovers	*þrumir*		

I, i

English	Old Norse
i	*ek, er, mér*
ice	*ís, ísi*
if	*ef, er*
ill	*ill, illa, illr, illrar, ills, illum*
ill-will	*læs*
in	*á, at, í, in, inn, innan, inni, inum*
informed	*nýsisk*
inquire	*fregna*
inside	*innar*
insults	*háðungar*
invite	*biðja*
invited	*boðit*
is	*á, er, sér*
is-not	*er-a, er-at*
it	*at, hann, þat*

J, j

English	Old Norse
joints	*liðum*
joy	*fögnuð, gaman*
joyful	*feginn*
joyful-conversation	*gamanrúnum*
joys	*gaman*
judgement	*dómr*

K, k

English	Old Norse
kettle	*katli*
killing	*víg*
kin	*nið, niðr*

Word List (*English to Old Norse*)

English	Old Norse	English	Old Norse
kingdom	*ríki*	limping	*haltr*
king's	*konungs*	listen	*hlýðir*
kinsmen	*frændr, frændum, kynnis*	listened	*hlýdda*
		little	*lítil, lítilla, lítit, litlu*
kiss	*kossa*	live	*lifa, lifir*
knees	*kné*	lives	*lifir*
know	*kann, kannt, váar, veit, vita, vitu, vitu*	living	*kvikr, lifa, lifðum*
		loaf	*hleif, hleifi*
knowing	*veit, vísum, vita, viti*	loath	*leiða*
knowing-not	*veit-a*	loathed	*leiðr*
known	*kannar, kuðr, veit, vitaðr, vitandi*	loathes	*leiðisk*
		locks	*lyki*
knows	*kann, veit*	loddfáfnir	*loddfáfnir*
knows-not	*kann-at*	logs	*skíða*
know-you	*veistu, veiztu*	long	*lengi, sitt*
		longest	*lengst*
		long-friends	*langvini*

L, l

		longing	*munr*
lacking	*vanr*	look	*líta, skoðar, skoðask*
laid	*lagið, lögðumk*	lose-sight-of	*firrask*
laments	*sýtir*	loudly	*æpandi*
land	*stað*	love	*ást, ástar, friðr, munuð, unna*
late	*síð*		
laugh	*hlæ, hlæja*	loved	*ann, ljúfr, ljúfum*
laughs	*hlær*	loyalty	*tryggðum*
laughter	*hlægis, hlátr, hlátri*	luck	*frama*
launch	*ýta*	lust	*löst*
launched	*ýta*		
lay	*láta*		

M, m

laying	*liggjandi*		
learn	*fregna*	made	*gerðu*
learning	*fregna*	maiden	*mær, mey*
less	*færa*	maiden's	*meyjar*
let	*lætr, lát, láttu, leitir, lét, létumk*	makes	*gerir*
		malice	*fár*
let-be	*er*	man	*firar, guma, gumi, hal, halr, karla, maðr, man, mann, mann, manna, manni*
lie	*lygi*		
lies	*flátt, liggja*		
life	*fjör*		
light-mother	*ljósa*	man's	*manni*
lights	*ljósum*	mankind	*öld*
like	*glík*	manly	*mannskis*
limbs	*boglimum*	man's	*guma, manns*

80

Word List (*English to Old Norse*)

English	Old Norse	English	Old Norse
man-sense	*mannvit*	mountains	*fjall, fjalli*
many	*fjölð, marga, margan, margir, margr, margt, mörg, mörgum*	mouth	*munn*
		much	*mikil, mikit, mjök*
		much-wise	*margfróðr*
married	*gefin*	my	*mik, minn, míns*
master	*halr*	myself	*sjalfr, sjalfum*
matter	*mæla, mál*		
may	*má, mætti, mega, megi, megu*		

N, n

English	Old Norse
me	*mér, mik*
mead	*mjaðar, mjöð*
meal	*verðar, verði, virði*	naked	*nökkviðr*
meals	*málungi*	named	*heitir*
meaningful	*ráðna*	nation	*þjóð*
measure	*mjöt*	nature	*aðal*
meats	*lær*	naught	*neiss*
men	*gumna, gumnar, manni, menn*	near	*nær, næst*
		nearer	*nær*
men's	*alda, guma, gumna, manna*	need	*nauðr, þörf, þurfu*
		needed	*þörf, þyrftak*
met	*mæti*	needles	*barr*
middle-wise	*meðalsnotr*	needs	*þörf, þyrfti*
might	*megin*	needy	*válaðs*
mighty	*máttki*	never	*æva, ævagi, aldregi, aldrei*
mighty-songs	*fimbulljóð*		
mild	*mildir*	new-formed	*einnættum*
mind	*geð, geði, geðs, hugar, hugi, hugr*	new-slain	*nýfelldum*
		night	*nótt*
mind-fickle	*hugbrigð*	nights	*nætr*
mindful	*minnigr*	nine	*níu*
minds	*geð*	ninth	*níunda*
mine	*mín, mína, mínar, minna, mínu*	no	*engi*
		no-end	*ósköp*
miserable	*vesall*	no-man	*manngi*
misfortune	*víti*	none	*eigi, einugi, engi, engu, manngi, öng*
mocking	*hæðinn*		
moderation	*hófi*	no-one	*engi, manngi*
money	*fé*	nor	*né*
month	*mánuði*	not	*eigi, ekki, engi, er-a, eyvitar, hittki, né, vættki*
mood	*æðis*		
moon	*mána*		
mope	*snópir*	not-asked	*óbeðit*
more	*fleira, meira*	noted	*notit*
morning	*morgin, morgni*	not-friends	*óvinar*
most	*mikilsti*	nothing	*ekki, vettki*

81

Word List (*English to Old Norse*)

English	Old Norse	English	Old Norse
not-sent	*ósent*		
no-use	*ónýtr*		
now	*nú*		

O, o

P, p

English	Old Norse	English	Old Norse
oak	*eik*	painted	*fáði*
ocean	*mar*	pasture	*beiti, grasi*
odin	*óðinn, óðni*	pay	*gjalda*
of	*á, að, af, at, eða, of, þanns, um*	payment	*gjöld*
		peace	*frið, friðr*
of-ale	*ölðri*	peer	*skyggnast*
off	*af*	peered	*nýsta*
offer	*bjóða*	people	*þjóða*
of-friend	*vinar*	place	*ey*
of-men's	*alda*	places	*staðar, staði*
of-mind	*geðs*	plains	*velli*
of-old	*aldar*	play	*leiki*
often	*oft*	playing-tricks	*leika*
old	*aldinn, aldna, gamlir*	play-trickery	*leiki*
on	*á, at*	plenty	*ærnu*
once	*forðum*	pole	*meiði*
one	*einir, einn, einum, eitt, hverr*	poured	*ausinn*
		powers-gods	*ginnregin*
one's	*eins*	praise	*leyfa, lof, lofi*
only	*eitt*	pressed	*ýta*
or	*eða, né*	pride	*metnaðr*
origin	*rök*	proved	*reynda*
other	*hitt, öðrum, órir*	provisions	*nesti*
others	*öðrum*		
othrorir	*óðreri, óðrerir*		

Q, q

English	Old Norse
out	*er*
out-of	*á, ór*
outside	*út, úti*
over	*á, yfir*
over-aled	*ofrölvi*
over-drinking	*ofdrykkja*
over-sacrificed	*ofblótit*
over-used	*ofsóit*
owned	*eigi*
owns	*eiga*

English	Old Norse
quarrel	*vrekask*
questioned	*freginn*
quickens	*kveikisk*
quiet	*kyrri*
quote	*kveða*
quoted	*kveða*

R, r

English	Old Norse
raise	*reisi, ríða, ríst*
raised	*reist*
rather	*haldendr, heldr*
rati	*rata*

Word List (*English to Old Norse*)

English	Old Norse	English	Old Norse
raw	*hrás*	sacrifice	*blóta*
realm	*görðum*	safe	*heilir*
realms	*væra*	sage	*þul*
received	*þegit*	said	*kvað, kveðr, segja*
receivers-of-gifts	*endrgefendr*	same	*sama, senn*
receives	*þægi*	sands	*sanda*
recited	*kveðin*	sat	*sat*
redeemed	*keypts*	save	*bjarga*
reeds	*reyri*	save-i-not	*bjargig-a-k*
regard	*líknstafi*	saw	*sá*
reindeer	*hrein*	say	*segir, segja*
repaid	*gjöld*	says	*segir, segja*
repayment	*laun*	sea	*sæ, sævar, sjó*
rest	*ro*	seas	*sæva*
returned	*aftr*	season	*misseri*
reward	*gjalda, gjöld, iðgjöld*	second	*annat*
rewards	*laun*	secrecy	*dul*
rich	*auðigr*	see	*sé, sék, sjá*
riches	*auði, aurum*	seeds	*frævask*
rides	*ríði, ríðr*	seek	*séir*
rigidly	*stinnt*	seeks	*fiðr*
ring	*baug*	seem	*þykkisk*
ring-oath	*baugeið*	seemed	*sýnst, þóttumk, þóttusk*
rise	*rísa*	seems	*þykkir, þykkisk*
rise-not	*rís-at*	seen	*sé, sýn*
roam	*ratar*	see-not	*sé-t*
roamed	*ratar*	seldom	*sjaldan*
rock	*grjót*	self	*sjalfr*
rootless	*rótlausum*	self-willed	*sjalfráða*
roots	*rótum, vrótum*	send	*senda*
rose	*reis*	serpent	*ormi*
rough-shoe	*óbryddum*	seventeenth	*sjautjánda*
round	*randir*	seventh	*sjaunda*
row	*róa*	shaft	*flein, skaft*
ruler's	*þjóðans*	shaftmaker	*skeftismiðr*
rules	*ræðr*	shall	*munt, skal, skalt, skaltu, skulu*
run	*renn*	shall-not	*skal-a*
runes	*rúnar, rúnum*	shall-not-you	*skal-at-tu*
rush	*vaða*	shall-you	*skaltu*
		shame	*skammisk*
		sharp	*skörpum*

S, s

Word List (English to Old Norse)

English	Old Norse	English	Old Norse
sharply	ofarla	some	suma, sumar, sumr, sumt
she	hon	somebody-else's	einhverjum
shelter	skyli	son	sonr, syni
shield	skjöld	songs	ljóð, ljóða
ship	skip	sons	mögr, sona, sonu, sonum, syni, synir
ships	skips	soon	brátt, snemma
shoe	skór	soothing	sefa
shoes	skúa	sorrow	sorg, sorgum, sút
shoesmith	skósmiðr	sorrowful	sorgafullr
short	skammar	sorrow-losing	sorgalausastr
shot	skotinn	sorrows	sútum
should	myndi, skyli	sought	leitaði, sótta
should-be	skulu, skyli	space	rúms
should-not	mun-at	spares	sparir
shouldn't	skyli-t	speak	mæla, mæli, mælum
sick	sjúkum	speaks	mæli, mælir
sickness	sótt, sóttum	spear	geiri, geirs
sight	sjónum	spears	geirar
silence	endrþögu, þegjandi	speech	mál, máli, máls
silent	þagalt, þagðak, þegi, þegir, þögðu, þögull, þruma, þrumir	spirit	geð, mun
since	því	spoke	mælta
sing	gala	spring	sprettr
sinks-not	hnígr-a	spying	njósn
sister	systir	staffs	velir
sit	sitja, str	stand	standa
sits	sitr	standing	stendr
sitting	sitr	stands	stendr
sixteenth	sextánda	staves	stafi
sixth	sétta, sétti	stay	stað
skin	belg, lær	steals	stelr
skins	hám, skrám	steer-less	stjórnlausu
slander	róg	steers	stýrir
slaughter	fjörlagi	sticks	stafi
sleep	sofa	stiff	stinna
sleeping	sefr, sofa, sofandi, sofin	still	enn
slept	svæfik	stingy	glöggvan
slipperiness	hálum	stocked	grindr
smoothed	glatt	stole	svikinn
snatching	snapir	stomach	maga, magi
so	sá, sé, sú, svá	stood	stóðumk
		stool	stóli

Word List (*English to Old Norse*)

English	*Old Norse*	English	*Old Norse*
stop-not	*stöðvig-a-k*	the-air	*lofti*
straight	*drjúgt*	the-brave	*fræknum*
strength	*afl*	the-field	*akri*
strike	*höggs, höggva*	the-great-thyle	*fimbulþulr*
strong	*líknfastan, rammt*	the-heart	*hjarta*
success	*sigr*	their	*sinna, þeim*
such	*slíkan, slíkt*	theirs	*síns, þeira*
sun	*sólar*	them	*þau, þeim, þeir*
sun-white	*sólhvíta*	themselves	*sjalfum*
sup	*sylg*	then	*at, þá, þann*
suspicion	*grunr*	the-only	*einna*
suttung	*suttung, suttungr*	there	*þar, þars, þeirar*
suttung's	*suttungs*	these	*þessa, þessu*
swine	*svíni*	the-way	*leið*
sword	*mæki, sverði*	the-wise	*horskum, snotrum*
swords	*hjörum*	they	*þær, þeim, þeir, þeira, þeiri, þeirs*
		thieves	*þjófar*

T, t

English	*Old Norse*	English	*Old Norse*
		thin	*magran*
tail	*hali*	think	*hygg, hyggja, hyggjum*
take	*nem, nema, nemir, nemr, taka*	thinks	*hyggr, hyggsk, þykkisk*
taken	*nema*	third	*þriðja, þrimr*
takes	*tekr*	thirteenth	*þrettánda*
talk	*segja, senna*	this	*er, í, það, þann, þess*
talkative	*málugr*	this-one	*hinn*
talks	*þylsk*	thjodrerir	*þjóðrerir*
tamed	*tamr*	those	*þeim*
tarnished	*saurgan*	though	*en, þó, þótt*
teach	*kennik*	thought	*hugar, hugat, hugðak, hugi, hyggjandi, hyggju, þótti, þóttumk*
tell	*telja*		
tempt	*teygðu*	thoughtful	*hugalt*
tempted	*teygða*	thoughts	*hug, hyggja*
tenth	*tíunda*	thrall	*þræli*
tested	*freista, reynt*	three	*þrír*
than	*en, er*	throw	*verpa*
that	*at, en, er, sá, þann, þat, þats, þeim*	thrown-not	*fýgr-a*
		thundr	*þundr*
thatched	*taugreftan*	tilted	*höllu*
that-one	*þann*	tired	*leiðr, móðr*
thawed-fell	*þáfjalli*	to	*á, at, í, til, við*
the	*á, at, er, in, inn, innar, ins, inum, it, þat*	to-be	*vera*
		to-beasts	*gjalti*

Word List (*English to Old Norse*)

English	Old Norse	English	Old Norse
to-bed	*beðjum*	uneasy	*ódælla*
together	*saman*	unfailing	*óbrigðra*
to-have	*höfði*	un-good	*ógótt*
to-her	*henni*	unknowing	*eyvitu*
to-me	*mér*	unknown	*ókunnum, ókynnis*
tongue	*tunga*	unlaid	*ólagat*
too	*of, til*	unless	*nema*
took	*nam*	unliving	*ólifðum*
to-one	*einum*	unlock	*upploki*
too-wary	*ofvaran*	un-lucky	*óhöpp*
to-receive	*þiggja*	un-needed	*óþörf*
to-speak	*þylja*	unreliable	*brigðum*
to-the-wary	*vörum*	unsheltered	*þöll*
towards	*ýta*	un-smart	*ósnjallr*
towel	*þerru*	unstable	*staðlausu, valtastr*
to-you	*sér, þér*	unsurely	*ógörla*
travel	*far, fara, fari, ferr*	until	*unz*
travelled	*farit, fór*	un-wealthy	*óauðigr*
travelling	*farinn*	unwise	*ósnotr, ósnotrs, ósviðr, ósvinna*
tree	*þorpi, tré, viðar, viði*		
tricked	*brigð*	un-wise	*ósnotr*
tried	*reyndr*	up	*upp, uppi*
trodden	*treðr*	use	*nýt, nýta, sóa*
trouble	*víl*	used	*nytak*
true		useful-like	*nytsamligt*
true			
trust	*trúa, trúi, trúir*	**V, v**	
trusting	*tryggr*		
truth	*sanna*	vessel	*keri*
try	*freista*	vestments	*váðir, váðum, væddr*
tuned	*þunnu*	vice	*löst*
turn	*hverfi*	vigorous	*hvatastr*
turning	*hverfanda*	villains	*fári*
twelfth	*tolfta*		
two	*tvær, tvau, tveim, tveir*	**W, w**	
two-year-old	*tvévetrum*		
		waited	*vættak*
U, u		wanting	*vant*
		war-descendents	*hildings*
uncertain	*óvíst*	wares	*vegnest*
under	*und, undir*	wariest	*varastr*
understand	*skil*	warmed-not	*hlýr-at*

Word List (*English to Old Norse*)

English	*Old Norse*	English	*Old Norse*
warriors	*fyrðar, rekkar, vígdrótt*	will-not	*vill-at*
wary	*gætinn, varan, vari*	willow	*viði, vill*
was	*væri, var, var, vark, vera*	wind	*byr, vind, vindi*
washed	*þveginn*	windy	*vindga*
watch	*hverr*	wins	*dugir*
water	*vatni, vatns*	wisdom	*fróðr, horska*
waters	*báru*	wise	*fróða, fróðr, fróðra, fróðum, horska, horskan, horskr, skilin, snotr, snotrs, sviðr, svinna*
wave	*vági*		
wavering	*váfir*		
waving	*váfa*		
waxing	*vaxanda*	wise-man's	*þular*
way	*brautu, vegr, vegum*	wise-men	*fróðra*
wayfarer	*ganganda*	wit	*vit*
ways	*vega, vegir*	witch	*völu*
we	*vér*	witchcraft	*fjölkynngi*
weakly	*seint*	with	*með, við, vit*
wealth	*auðr, fé, féar*	withered	*hrörnar*
wealthy	*auðgum, auðigr*	with-laughs	*viðhlæjendr*
weapons	*vápn, vápnum*	without	*án, vanr*
weather	*veðr, veðri, viðrir*	wit-less	*veit-a*
well	*vel*	wits	*vits*
well-of-urd	*urðarbrunni*	woeful-path	*vílstígr*
went	*gengu, varð*	wolf	*ulfi, ulfr*
wept	*grætta*	woman	*fljóð, kona, konu, konum*
were	*var, vár, váru*	woman's	*fljóðs, konu*
what	*er, hvat*	women	*kvenna*
wheel	*hvéli*	won	*unnit*
when	*at, en, er, hvars, nær*	wonder	*kyns*
where	*hvaðan, hvar, hvars*	wood	*við, viðar*
which	*er, hvers, hvert*	wooden-men	*trémönnum*
while	*meðan*	words	*mælir, orð, orða, orði, orðs, orðum*
white-armed	*hvítarmri*	work	*orka, verk, verka, verki, vinnask, vinnk*
who	*er, hveim*		
whole	*heila, öllum*	workers	*yrkjendr*
whose	*er, hverrar, hvers*	works	*verks, verkum*
widely	*víða*	worries	*hyggr*
wife	*kona, konu, vífs*	worse	*verr, verra, verri*
wild	*dýra, óðum, villr*	worsens	*versnar*
will	*mun, munu, vil, vildu, vilja, vill, vilt*	worth	*virði*
		worth-givers	*viðrgefendr*
willed	*vilja, vill*	would	*mundu, munu*
willing	*hvötum*		

Word List (*English to Old Norse*)

English	Old Norse
wouldn't	*væri-t*
wounded	*undaðr*
wounds	*særir*
wrong	*rangt*

Y, y

yards	*ráar*
yawning	*gínanda*
yet	*auk, enn*
yet-not	*þeygi*
you	*þér, þik, þitt, þú*
young	*ungan, ungr*
your	*þik, þínum*
yours	*þínum*
yourself	*sjalfr, sjalfum*
youthful	*manunga*

www.ingramcontent.com/pod-product-compliance
Lightning Source LLC
Chambersburg PA
CBHW051421070526
44584CB00023B/3523